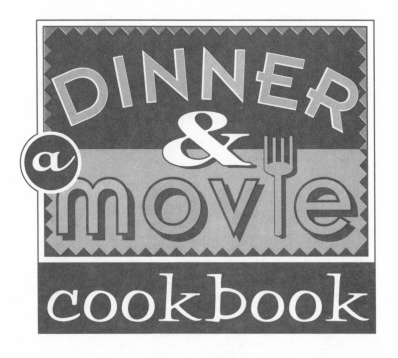

Recipes by Claud Mann

With Illustrations by Robert Clyde Anderson

Written by Kimberlee Carlson, Claud Mann & Robert Taylor

Turner Publishing, Inc.
ATLANTA

Library of Congress Cataloging-in-Publication Data

Dinner & a movie cookbook.
p. cm.
Includes index.
ISBN 1-57036-383-8 (alk. paper)
1. Cookery. 2. Motion pictures—Plots, themes, etc. I. Turner Publishing, Inc.
II. Dinner & a movie (Television program)
TX652.D5574 1996
641.5—dc20   96-25118
CIP

Published by Turner Publishing, Inc.
A Subsidiary of Turner Broadcasting System, Inc.
1050 Techwood Drive, N.W.
Atlanta, Georgia 30318

First Edition 10 9 8 7 6 5 4 3 2 1

Distributed by Andrews and McMeel
A Universal Press Syndicate Company
4900 Main Street
Kansas City, Missouri 64112

Printed in the United States of America

Dedicated to Mr. Limpett I
June 19, 1995 - November 30, 1995
& to the Blenderheads

Contents

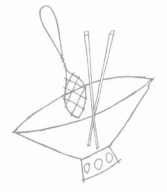

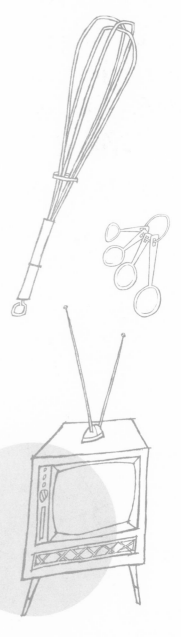

Where to Find What You Want

Dishes by Category

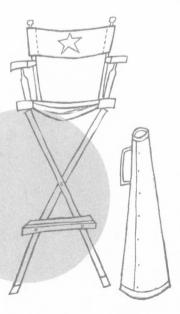

Sometimes an idea just seems right—
like cookies & milk, like barbeque & slaw,
like reindeer & lingonberries.
Like Dinner & a Movie on the Superstation TBS.

Right out of the oven, the show was a natural.
Let a favorite film inspire some good food, and then
whip it all up while watching the movie.

Thanks to the deliciously dry enthusiasm of our
hosts Paul Gilmartin and Annabelle Gurwitch, along
with the comic and culinary talents of producers
Kimberlee Carlson, Claud Mann, Ashley Evans,
Ward McCarthy, and Jack Pendarvis, we've created
prime-time television good enough to eat.

We now proudly present the first
Dinner & a Movie Cookbook. The best of our show
rolled into one toothsome book, so you can have
your dinner and a movie and eat it, too.

TBS cooks on Friday Nights!

Bon Appétit!

Kelly Cole
Executive in charge of Production

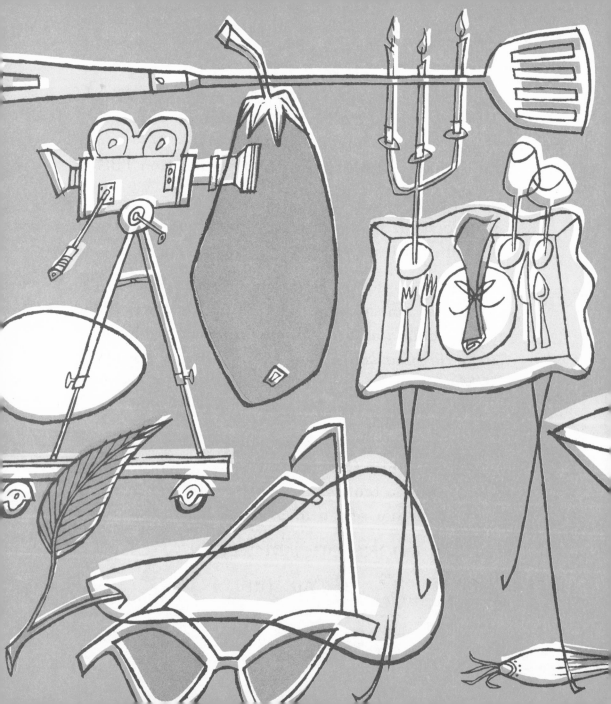

Love
At First
Bite

"Really Cheesy" Deep-Dish Lasagne

When we left off last time, the tomato sauce had entered the baking dish just in time to find the wild mushroom béchamel lying on top of the eggplant. What the eggplant didn't know was that the béchamel was just using it to get to the pasta. And now please join us for "As the Lasagne Layers."

Food for Thought

How to have a "Cheesy Moment"©

Don't let those onion-chopping tears go to waste. While wistfully remembering your sordid past, whimper stoically, working yourself into an uncontrollable frenzy so that someone else has to take over for you. Being careful with your mascara, use a dish towel to dry your eyes.

For the Tomato Sauce

2 Tbsp olive oil
½ onion, finely diced
5 cloves garlic, minced
3 lbs ripe tomatoes, peeled and
  chopped (or 1 28-oz can crushed
  Italian tomatoes)
Salt and pepper

For the Wild Mushroom Béchamel

3 cups milk
4 Tbsp butter, divided
½ lb mixed wild mushrooms, sliced
  (chanterelles, shiitake, portabello, etc.)
3 Tbsp flour
¼ tsp salt
⅛ tsp white pepper

For the Eggplant

2 lbs Japanese eggplant,
  cut lengthwise in ½-inch slices
2 Tbsp extra virgin olive oil
5 cloves garlic, finely chopped
½ tsp salt

¼ tsp black pepper
2 Tbsp finely chopped parsley

Now for the Really Cheesy Part

1 cup grated Pecorino Romano cheese
1½ cups grated mozzarella cheese
1½ cups grated provolone cheese
1 cup ricotta cheese
1 egg
Pinch of nutmeg
Salt and pepper
4 Tbsp thinly sliced fresh basil
Collected musical works of John Tesh

For the Pasta

1½ lbs fresh pasta sheets or 1 16-oz
  box dry lasagne noodles, cooked
  according to package instructions
1 can of wind-tunnel tested,
  super-hold hair spray, unisex
1 bottle Man-Tan, industrial strength
1 copy *A Daytime Actor Prepares*
  by Stanislavsky

- **Make the tomato sauce:** Heat the olive oil in a medium saucepan over medium heat. Add the onion and sauté until soft and translucent, about 5 minutes. Add the garlic and sauté another minute or two. Add tomatoes and simmer, uncovered, until the sauce just begins to thicken, about 20 minutes for fresh tomatoes (5–10 minutes if using canned tomatoes). Season to taste with salt and pepper.
- **Make the wild mushroom béchamel:** In a medium saucepan, on medium-low heat, bring the milk to a simmer. Do not boil.
- In a separate, heavy-bottomed saucepan, melt half the butter over medium-high heat, add the sliced mushrooms, and sauté for about 5 minutes, until softened. Remove mushrooms and set aside. In the same pan, melt remaining butter over a low flame; add the flour and cook without browning for about 2 minutes, stirring constantly. Whisk the hot milk into the butter-and-flour mixture a few tablespoons at a time, fully incorporating before adding more. Once all the milk has been added, stir and simmer over a low heat until creamy, about 10 minutes. Stir in the sautéed mushrooms, salt, and white pepper and set aside in a warm spot.
- **Cook the eggplant:** Preheat the broiler. Combine the olive oil, garlic, salt, and pepper. Arrange the eggplant slices on a cookie sheet, brush with the oil mixture, and broil until golden brown, about 5 minutes on each side, depending on the intensity of the broiler. Toss with the parsley and set aside.
- **Prepare the cheeses:** Toss together the three grated cheeses and set aside. Mix the ricotta with the egg, nutmeg, basil, and a pinch of salt and pepper and set aside.
- **Assemble the dish:** Preheat oven to 375°F. Grease a 9x13–inch baking dish with butter; then spread ½ cup of the béchamel and ¼ cup of the tomato sauce evenly over the bottom followed by: (1) pasta sheets (2) 1 cup tomato sauce (3) pasta sheets (4) half of the eggplant (5) 1 cup tomato sauce (6) 1 cup of grated cheese (7) pasta sheets (8) the ricotta mixture (9) pasta sheets (10) the remaining tomato sauce (11) the second half of the eggplant (12) 1 cup of cheese (13) pasta sheets (14) the remaining mushroom béchamel (15) the remaining cheese.
- Bake until the cheese on top begins to turn light brown and the sauce bubbles around the edges, about 25–30 minutes. Let cool 5–10 minutes before cutting. Yield: 8 servings.
- **Tip:** If you are currently suffering from amnesia, have one of your guests (perhaps the secret lover of your ex's fiance's evil twin) help keep track when you are layering all those fillings.

Chew on This

- It took the combined talents of Whoopie Goldberg, Kevin Kline, Sally Field, Robert Downey, Jr., Garry Marshall, Elisabeth Shue, Carrie Fisher, Cathy Moriarty, and Terry Hatcher to make *Soapdish*.

- It takes 2,500 pounds of milk to make 200 pounds of cheese.

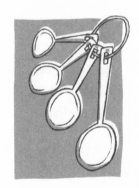

Young-and-Naked Fish Kabobs with Mango Tiki Sauce

Light the torches, sharpen your spears, and dive into the tropical innocence of a dinner that can be made with virtually no modern tools or restrictive clothing.

For the Mango Tiki Sauce

2 medium mangos, cut in chunks, or 1 cup frozen mango
2 Tbsp soy sauce
4 Tbsp dry sherry
¼ cup brown sugar
¼ cup cider vinegar
1 Tbsp peanut oil
2 cloves garlic, thinly sliced
2 tsp freshly grated ginger
¼ medium white onion, thinly sliced

For the Young-and-Naked Kabobs

1–2 lbs mahi-mahi (if unavailable, substitute swordfish, shark, or fresh tuna)
2 small zucchini
1 red onion
2 bell peppers
½ fresh pineapple
2 firm, ripe papayas
1 basket cherry tomatoes
3 Tbsp olive oil
Salt and pepper
2 scallions, thinly sliced on the diagonal
1 skimpy loincloth
1 roll Scotch tape (to affix long hair modestly to "bumpies")

**SKEWER TIP
#8**

Keep your skewers from burning up during broiling by first soaking them in water.

- **Mango Tiki Sauce:** In the bowl of a food processor or blender, combine the mango, soy sauce, sherry, brown sugar, and cider vinegar; blend to a smooth puree.
- Heat the peanut oil in a medium saucepan, over medium heat. Add the garlic, ginger, and onion and stir-fry for 1 minute (being careful not to burn). Add the pureed mango mixture and bring to a boil. Reduce heat and simmer for 10 minutes. Thin with a little island springwater if desired.
- **Kabob Construction:** Preheat broiler (the part of the stove you rarely use and are probably storing lids in). Pretend you are Christopher Atkins, spearfishing in clear, tropical waters, while Brooke waits shyly in the hut. Using separate bowls to hold each item: cut the mahi-mahi into 2-inch chunks; cut the zucchini, red onion, bell peppers, pineapple, and papayas into 1-inch pieces; leave cherry tomatoes whole.
- Spear kabob ingredients in sequence until each skewer is loaded with colorful trophies. Brush lightly with olive oil; season with salt and pepper; and place on a foil-lined broiler tray.
- Broil the kabobs for a total of 10 minutes, rotating a few times to brown evenly. For the last minute of cooking, brush on a little of the mango tiki sauce. When done, arrange the fish kabobs on a platter (or banana leaf) and spoon sauce over the top. Garnish with scallions and start the luau. Yield: 4 servings.
- Employ the spent and empty skewers as your own form of currency to barter favor from your fellow castaways. Or better yet, get them to do the dishes. Aloha!

Chew on This

MANGO TIP #34

One way to tell if a mango is ripe is the presence of oozing or weeping near the stem. If this condition exists on anything but your mango, there's a strong possibility that more than two of you are on the island.

Food for Thought

Question: **Where was the lipstick tree?** Answer: **Right next to the blow-dryer bush.**

Extra-Terrestrial Tempura

More mouthwatering than an alien autopsy, more satisfying than a nicely chilled alien probe, more astonishing than a blinding beam of multicolored light hovering above your pickup truck as you drive down a long, dark stretch of deserted highway somewhere north of Las Vegas . . . Be prepared to have your tastebuds abducted.

SCIENCE SAFETY TIP:

If your fryer is equipped with a Kleistron tube, never let the oil rise above 360°F. (Ruining a batch of tempura is one thing, but destroying the atmosphere of a neighboring galaxy is universally considered very poor form in anyone's cookbook.)

For the Tempura
8 jumbo shrimp
1 sweet potato, peeled and
    cut into ½-inch rounds
1 yellow onion, halved lengthwise and
    cut into 1-inch slices
10 medium mushrooms, stems trimmed
1 Japanese eggplant, sliced on the
    diagonal in 1-inch slices
10 green beans, cleaned and trimmed
1 bunch green onions, trimmed and
    cut in half
1 canned lotus root, cut on the
    diagonal into thin slices (optional)

For the Dipping Sauce
⅓ cup sake (or Japanese mirin
    cooking wine, if available)
⅓ cup light soy sauce
1 cup water
1 cup clam juice (or Japanese
    dashi, if available)
1 tsp sugar
1 Tbsp fresh ginger, grated
2 Tbsp red radish, grated (or Japanese
    daikon, if available)

**For the Oil and Batter
(makes three batches)**
½ cup sesame oil
3 cups soy oil
3 egg yolks, beaten
3 cups ice water
3½ cups all-purpose flour
1 copy *Men Are From Mars,
    Women Are From Venus*

- **Prepare the shrimp:** Shell and devein the shrimp, leaving the tails on. Make 3 or 4 small incisions (¼-inch) on the inside of each shrimp to prevent curling as they fry. Rinse in cold water, dry with paper towels, and set aside.
- **Prepare the vegetables:** Dry the cut vegetables well; arrange on a tray or platter.

- **Prepare the dipping sauce:** In a small saucepan, bring the sake to a boil. Ignite with a match and shake gently while the alcohol burns off. Add the soy sauce, water, clam juice, and sugar and return to a boil. Remove from heat, cover, and keep warm.
- **Prepare the oil:** In a large, heavy saucepan or deep fryer, combine the sesame and soy oils and heat to a temperature of 340–360°F. (Test the oil temperature by dripping a few drops of batter into the oil. If the oil is hot enough, the batter will sink partially, then rise very quickly to the top.)
- **Prepare the batter in three batches:** In a medium mixing bowl, lightly mix 1 egg yolk with 1 cup of the ice water. Add 1 cup of the flour all at once and *fold* the flour into the egg mixture with just a few strokes until the ingredients are barely combined. ***Important:*** The batter should remain very lumpy. If mixed until smooth the result will be a thick, heavy coating.
- **Set up an assembly line:** Arrange all tools and ingredients from left to right around the cooking area as follows: a) *dry* shrimp and vegetables to be fried; b) remaining sifted flour; c) tempura batter; d) hot oil; e) slotted spoon and chopsticks; f) draining rack or paper towels.
- **Fry the tempura:** Each piece of food to be fried should be dredged in flour, with the excess shaken off; dipped quickly in the batter; and fried 2–3 minutes until golden, turning once in the oil. Remove from the oil with a slotted spoon or chopsticks and drain briefly before serving. Use the batter as quickly as possible, mixing more only as it is needed.
- **Eat:** Add the ginger and radish to the dipping sauce. Dip each piece of hot and crispy tempura into the sauce and consume. If your mission went as planned, it should be as crisp as a crop circle and taste out of this world. Yield: 2 servings.

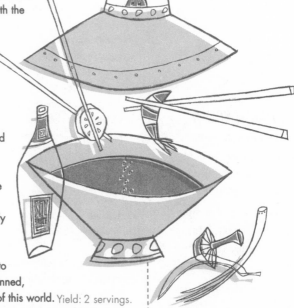

Food for Thought   As an advanced being from an alien culture, why does Kim Basinger still have to carry a purse?

ALIEN TIP
#224
If you ever have an alien sighting, call UFO central at 1-800-350-4639. Operators are standing by.

"Goin' to the Chapel" Chicken Rollups

Whether you're a friend of the bride or the groom, you'll love our savory spin on the dreaded rubber banquet chicken served at weddings everywhere.

For the Stuffing
1 Tbsp olive oil
3 cloves garlic, peeled and crushed
2 sweet Italian sausages,
    skinned and chopped
1 medium onion, finely chopped
1/4 cup pine nuts
1/4 cup golden raisins
1/3 cup bread crumbs
2 Tbsp Italian parsley, minced
1/4 cup sour cream
1/3 cup grated Parmesan cheese
1/8 tsp red pepper flakes
1/4 tsp fresh rosemary, finely chopped

For the Chicken
6 half chicken breasts,
    boned (skinned, optional)
Kosher salt
Freshly ground black pepper

3 Tbsp butter, melted
3 Tbsp grated Parmesan cheese
3 Tbsp bread crumbs
2 tsp paprika
1/2 cup champagne
1/2 cup chicken stock
2 Tbsp cold butter, cut into small pieces
8 dozen handkerchiefs

Suggested Accompaniments
Broiled tomatoes
Blanched asparagus
1 unidentifiable rice dish
200 gallons of water, frozen solid
    and skillfully sculpted into the
    TBS logo, to be displayed proudly in
    center of table
1 roomful of distant relatives you've
    never met

- **Chicken, do you take this stuffing?** In a medium skillet, heat olive oil and garlic on medium heat until garlic just begins to turn a pale gold. Add the sausage and sauté for 10 minutes; transfer meat to a plate and set aside.
- Add the onions to the hot skillet and cook 5 minutes until tender and translucent. Add the pine nuts and raisins and continue cooking 2–3 minutes, stirring often. Remove skillet from heat and allow to cool a little.

INSIDE SCOOP
Don't waste money buying breadcrumbs when you can make them yourself. Keep leftover bread scraps in the freezer. When you need breadcrumbs, toast the scraps in the oven at 250°F until dry, then grind them in a food processor.

- In a medium mixing bowl, combine the bread crumbs, parsley, sour cream, Parmesan cheese, red pepper flakes, and rosemary. Add the sausage and the onion mixture and set aside.
- *Stuffing, do you take this chicken?* Preheat oven to 450°F. Rinse and pat chicken dry. One by one, place each breast between 2 sheets of plastic wrap and pound out as flatly and as evenly as possible with a meat pounder (or flat side of another heavy object). Arrange the flattened breasts skin-side down (or smooth-side, if skinless) on a work surface and season lightly with salt and pepper.
- Divide the sausage mixture evenly among the breasts and roll up as tightly as possible. Fasten with a toothpick or wooden skewer. Arrange the stuffed breasts seam-side down on a buttered baking dish; brush with melted butter and sprinkle evenly with Parmesan cheese, bread crumbs, and paprika. Pour the champagne and chicken stock around rollups.
- Bake in the upper third of the 450°F oven for 5 minutes; reduce the heat to 325°F and continue baking 20–25 minutes.
- *Procreating the sauce:* Remove rollups to a warm platter and cover. Pour the pan juices into a small saucepan and boil until reduced by half; remove saucepan from heat and whisk in the cold butter.
- *By the powers vested in me by Cordon Bleu . . . :* Ceremoniously ask your guests whether or not anyone objects to this tasty union of chicken and stuffing. If not, cut chicken into 1-inch slices and carefully transfer to plates. Spoon a little sauce over and give away at once. Yield: 4–6 servings.

BRIDESMAID'S DRESS TIP
#24 & 25

Don't know what to do with those stunning dresses in your closet? How about sewing them together to make a tastefully understated circus tent or even a hot air balloon? Nothing celebrates the sanctity of marriage better than the holy union of apricot and chartreuse.

Teen Angst Classics

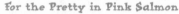

Pretty in Pink Salmon Filets

Do you dress kind of funny? Live on the wrong side of the tracks? Mom on the lam? Dad look like Harry Dean Stanton? Relax; once the hateful, jaded, snobby rich kids discover that you've mastered cold poached salmon, you're IN!

For the Pretty in Pink Salmon
4 6-oz skinless, boneless salmon filets
1½ quarts water
2 cups white wine
1 lemon, cut in half
1 carrot, sliced
2 bay leaves
5 black peppercorns
2 tsp salt
6 leeks, green tops trimmed and halved lengthwise

For the Virgin Tomato Sauce
1 lb very ripe tomatoes
1 Tbsp rice wine vinegar
½ tsp Dijon mustard
2 Tbsp of the salmon poaching liquid
2 tsp fresh tarragon, chopped
4 Tbsp extra virgin olive oil
Salt and pepper
1 quart teen angst
1 groovster prom dress, fashioned from foil, napkins, and clingwrap

- **Prepare the salmon:** Rinse the salmon filets in cold water. Run a finger down the center of the filet to feel for any remaining pin bones and remove if necessary. (A small pair of tweezers or needle-nose pliers can be used.) Combine the water, white wine, lemon, carrot, bay leaves, peppercorns, and salt in a large

Chew on This

When poaching meat or fish, the single most important thing to remember is to never allow the poaching liquid to come to a boil.

saucepan. Bring to a boil, reduce heat, and simmer 5–10 minutes, until fragrant. To poach, lower the leeks and salmon filets gently into the simmering liquid and cover; cook without boiling for 5 minutes, until the flesh of the fish is no longer translucent. Remove pan from heat and keep covered until cool. Once cool, transfer the filets and leeks to a plate, cover them, and refrigerate.

- **Make the Virgin Tomato Sauce:** Drop whole tomatoes into boiling water for 10 seconds, then drop immediately into ice-cold water. The peel can now be easily pulled off with the fingers. Cut the peeled tomato in half crosswise and firmly squeeze out the seeds. Chop the peeled, seeded tomatoes as finely as possible, either by hand or with a few pulses of a food processor. In a medium-sized mixing bowl, whisk together the tomatoes, vinegar, mustard, poaching liquid, and tarragon. Slowly whisk the olive oil into the tomato mixture little by little until well emulsified. Season with salt and pepper to taste.

- **To serve:** Slice the reserved leeks into thin strips and pile on each plate. Place chilled salmon over the leeks and spoon a little sauce over the top. Yield: 4 servings.

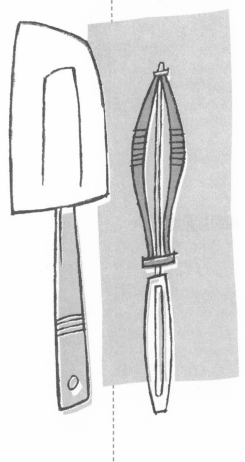

Food for Thought

Molly Ringwald was offered
Laura Dern's role in
Blue Velvet but turned it down
at the advice of her mother,
who thought it was just
about bugs and S & M.

The Breakfast Club Sandwich

Finally, a sandwich that understands your desperate need for individuality. Who cares what the adults say; they don't listen to you anyway. You can have a sandwich for breakfast on a Friday night if you want to. Remember, we're all in this together.

You Will Need (But What About My Needs?)
4 slices thick-cut bacon, salty as one's own tears
1 tsp freshly cracked black pepper
1 Tbsp butter
1 Tbsp finely chopped onion
¼ cup thinly sliced red bell pepper
2 large eggs, beaten
Salt and pepper
1 tsp fresh basil, very thinly sliced
3 Tbsp grated mozzarella
3 thick slices sourdough bread
3 Tbsp mayonnaise
½ avocado, sliced
1 ripe tomato, sliced
1 handful watercress
Self-pity, to taste

- Preheat oven to 375°F. While the oven heats up, so can you. Take a few minutes to whine about anything that your parents ever did or didn't do that might have stunted your emotional or spiritual growth.
- Lay bacon out on a cookie sheet and sprinkle with the cracked black pepper. Bake for 10–15 minutes until crisp, turning once. Remove from oven and set aside. (Leave oven on.)
- Melt butter in a small nonstick sauté pan over medium heat. When the butter

Food for Thought
EGG TIP
#879
If uncertain as to whether or not an egg is fresh, drop it in salted water. If it floats, it's probably time to buy new eggs.

begins to bubble, add the onion and bell pepper and sauté until tender, about a minute.

- Pour the beaten eggs into the center of the hot pan. Cook for a minute without stirring to let the sides and bottom set. Using a spatula or fork, pull the cooked egg away from the sides while tilting the pan to let any raw egg run down to the hot bottom. Season the fritatta with salt, pepper, and fresh basil and top with grated mozzarella. Transfer the pan to the hot oven and bake for 3 minutes.
- Remove crusts from bread if desired (depending upon which character you most identify with) and toast lightly.
- Set out the remaining ingredients and begin constructing the sandwich from the bottom up: Start with one slice of toast and spread mayonnaise on the top side. Add the fritatta and the avocado slices. Spread both sides of the second piece of toast with a little mayo and lay that over the avocado. Next comes the peppered bacon, tomato slices, and watercress. Spread the last, but no less important, piece of toast with a little mayonnaise and place firmly, but sensitively, over that bitter and often misunderstood watercress.
- Viciously spear the layers together at each corner to vent any remaining teenage aggression. Cut diagonally into quarters and remember that, like all of us, each quarter contains a little bit of everything. . . . Yield: 2 servings.

INSIDE SCOOP
Did you know that this was the movie that gave birth to the Brat Pack?

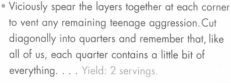

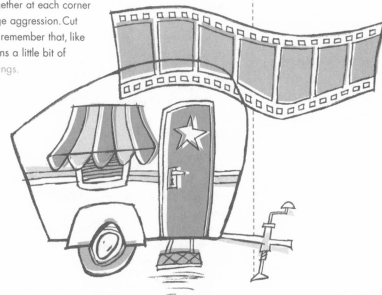

Chew on This

This is not a "heart smart" meal, so do what Emilio Estevez does in this movie and run through your local high school library pumping your fists in the air for 20 minutes daily, or until you're thrown out.

"Pony Boy" Fries
& "Cherry Valance" Pie

In this stylized Francis Ford Coppola production of S. E. Hinton's brooding tale, truants are living on their own and on the run. Lucky for us, you don't have to be a runaway to enjoy this "Classic Unsupervised Adolescent Fare."®

For the Pie Crust
2½ cups flour
½ tsp salt
1 Tbsp sugar
6 Tbsp chilled vegetable shortening, cut in ¼-inch cubes
8 Tbsp chilled unsalted butter, cut in ¼-inch cubes
5–7 Tbsp ice water
1 egg white, lightly beaten

For the Pie Filling
1 tsp freshly ground cinnamon
1 cup sugar
2 Tbsp cornstarch

2 Tbsp quick-cooking tapioca
4–5 cups sour cherries, drained
½ cup cherry juice
⅛ tsp almond extract
1 Tbsp fresh lemon juice
2 Tbsp butter

For the Fries
5 mature russet potatoes
Canola oil, as needed
Salt
Chili powder
1 switchblade-style pie knife
1 copy *Gone With the Wind*

- **Pie crust:** In a medium bowl, mix together the flour, salt, and sugar. Add the shortening and, using a pastry blender or two knives, work it into the flour until it resembles coarse cornmeal. Cut in butter until the bits are no larger than small peas.
- Sprinkle ice water onto the mixture one tablespoon at a time, mixing with a fork after each addition to moisten the dough evenly. The amount of ice water needed may vary according to the humidity or the brand of flour used. Using your hands,

first gently shape the dough into 2 balls; then flatten into 5-inch discs. Wrap in plastic and refrigerate 30 minutes.

- **For the filling:** Mix together the cinnamon, sugar, cornstarch, and tapioca. Add the cherries, cherry juice, almond extract, and lemon juice, and let stand 10 minutes.

- **Assemble the pie:** Preheat oven to 450°F. Roll out one piece of chilled dough to approximately 10 inches in diameter. Transfer dough to a buttered 9-inch pie plate and trim edges to leave ½-inch excess. Fold excess under itself. Lightly brush the inside of the crust with egg white. Pour filling into crust and dot with butter.

- Cut remaining pastry dough into 1-inch-wide strips and lay over the the filling in a criss-cross latticework. Trim excess, fold under, and flute the edges with a fork.

- Bake for 10 minutes in the lower third of the oven, reduce heat to 350°F, and continue baking another 45 minutes until the crust is golden brown.

- **Make the fries:** Scrub potatoes, peel (optional), and cut into strips 3 inches long and ⅜-inch square. Cover with cold water and let stand 10–20 minutes. Drain and dry well with paper towels.

- Fill deep-fat fryer or large saucepan with oil to a depth of 5–6 inches. Using a frying thermometer, slowly heat to a temperature of 300°–325°F.

- Fry potatoes in one- to two-cup batches until they just begin to turn a pale gold, about 2 minutes. Remove from oil with a slotted spoon and drain on paper towels in a single layer until cool to the touch.

- Raise oil temperature to 375°F and refry the blanched potatoes in small batches, moving them constantly until crisp and golden, about 3 minutes. (When no one is looking, take a minute and whisper to them "Stay crisp and golden, man.") Drain, toss with salt and chili powder, and serve at once. Yield: 8 servings.

Food for Thought

Never eat a lot of fries right before participating in a big rumble. They'll just slow you down and you'll probably need teeth for that cherry pie.

Suffering Succotash

So what if your high school teacher is dating your girlfriend, you just got fired from your pathetic job at Pig Burger, and the psychotic newspaper boy is stalking you for a measly $2. Don't end it all. What you need is a meal made just for you.

6 ears fresh corn
1 onion
2 bell peppers
3 large, ripe tomatoes
2 cups baby lima beans, fresh or frozen
4 skinless, boneless turkey thighs
Salt and pepper
4 Tbsp flour
4 Tbsp pure olive oil
½ tsp fresh sage, finely chopped
¼ cup dry sherry
2 cups chicken or turkey broth
1 lemon, cut into quarters
1 small reason to live

> **"Death is Nature's way of saying, 'Your table is ready.'"**
> —Robin Williams

Chew on This

Curtis Armstrong and John Cusack starred in another film directed by Savage Steve Holland, *One Crazy Summer*.

- Husk the corn, remove silk, and cut kernels from the cob into a mixing bowl. With the back of the knife blade, scrape the pulp from each cob into the bowl with the kernels.
- Dice the onion and bell peppers, quarter the tomatoes, and set aside. Blanch the lima beans until tender, about 15 minutes; rinse with cold water, drain, and set aside.
- Cut the turkey thighs into bite-sized chunks, season with a little salt and pepper, and toss with the flour.
- Heat 2 tablespoons of olive oil over medium-high heat in a heavy pot or Dutch oven. Add half of the turkey and sauté until golden brown, about 5 minutes.

Transfer the cooked turkey to a plate. Add the remaining olive oil to the pot and repeat with the remaining turkey. Transfer to a plate.

- Add onion, bell peppers, and sage to the hot pan and sauté a few minutes until the onions become soft and translucent. Add the sherry and reduce by half, scraping the pot with a wooden spoon to loosen tasty bits stuck to the bottom and sides.

- Return the turkey to the pot, add the chicken stock, and bring to a simmer. Cook covered for 30–45 minutes, or until the turkey is quite tender. Add the corn and corn pulp, lima beans, and tomatoes. Simmer, uncovered, an additional 5 minutes.

- Season with salt to taste, a generous grinding of black pepper, and a squeeze of lemon. Serve hot with rice.

- Get your head out of the oven, relight the pilot lights, and coil up any unused nooses. Dinner is served! Yield: 4–6 servings.

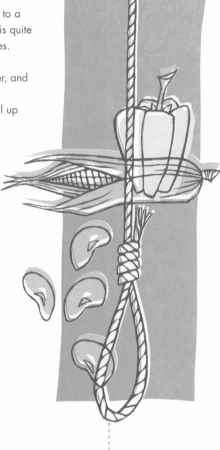

Did You Know:
LIMA BEAN TIP
#77
Raw lima beans contain small amounts of the toxin cyanide. Scary as it sounds, lima lovers need not despair. Cooking them uncovered in boiling water for as little as 10 minutes will remove any trace of those pesky poisonous compounds.

Heather's "Killer" Pasta with Oregano

Greetings and salutations. Most people think making fresh pasta is murder, but we suggest you give it a shot. It's not gonna kill ya, and you might find yourself the most popular person in your kitchen.

For the Sauce
4 Tbsp olive oil
½ cup dry red wine
3 Tbsp tomato paste
1 yellow onion, diced
8 garlic cloves, peeled and crushed
2 lbs ripe roma tomatoes, sliced in half lengthwise
1 tsp salt
½ tsp freshly ground black pepper

For the Pasta
4 cups unbleached, all-purpose flour
3 Tbsp fresh oregano, finely chopped
2 tsp salt
4 large eggs
Cold water, as needed
Parmesan cheese
1 copy *Moby-Dick*, dog-eared and underlined
1 big red scrunchie

- Preheat oven to 350°F. Mix together the olive oil, red wine, tomato paste, diced onions, and crushed garlic.

> **"What foods these morsels be."**
> —Glen Shadix (Father Ripper)

INSIDE SCOOP

To make an herb pasta, knead into the dough ½ cup of finely chopped herbs. For spinach pasta, substitute ½ cup of pureed frozen spinach for one of the eggs.

- Arrange the tomatoes cut-side up on a large cookie sheet. Drizzle the olive oil mixture over the tomatoes, season with salt and pepper, and roast for 35–45 minutes.
- Place flour, oregano, and salt in food processor. Turn on machine and add the eggs in a slow, steady stream. Continue processing until dough just begins to form a ball. Add a touch of water only if the dough hasn't begun to come together and still looks dry.
- Stop processor and feel the dough; it should hold together well but not be sticky. Transfer to a lightly floured surface and knead by hand another 10 minutes.
- Cover with a kitchen towel or plastic wrap and let the dough rest at least 15 minutes before proceeding.
- Divide pasta dough into three equal parts and roll to desired thickness either with a rolling pin or a hand-cranked pasta machine. Dust the pasta sheets with a little flour and let dry 5–10 minutes before cutting.

- Cut pasta by first dusting well with flour then rolling loosely into a cylinder and cutting crosswise at ⅛-inch intervals. Toss the cut pasta with a little flour to separate the strands and keep them from sticking together.
- Transfer the roasted tomatoes to a blender or food processor and puree until fairly smooth. Check and correct seasonings to taste, cover, and keep warm.
- Cook noodles in a large quantity of rapidly boiling, lightly salted water for about one minute, or until the pasta floats to the surface. Drain well and serve immediately with the roasted tomato sauce and loads of freshly grated Parmesan. Yield: 4 servings.
- Serve the meal to your hungry guests, and, regardless of gender, make everyone wear the big red scrunchies.

SAFETY TIP:
Show great caution when handling electric appliances, razor sharp knives, boiling water, etc. (Accidents are bound to happen.)

Fast Times at Ridgemont High *(1982)*

Sean Penne Pasta Salad

The year is 1982; kids are in the malls; the ubiquitous pasta salad is all the rage; and director Amy Heckerling is about to unleash Sean Penn on an unsuspecting public.

For the Dressing
½ cup pure olive oil
½ tsp crushed red pepper
Juice of one lemon
1 clove garlic, minced
2 tsp fresh dill, chopped
¼ tsp salt

For the Salad
8 oz penne pasta
½ cup Niçoise olives, roughly chopped
¼ cup cornichons, sliced
2 Tbsp capers
2 cups cherry tomatoes, quartered
1 red onion, thinly sliced
½ cup grated Romano cheese
¼ cup flat-leaf parsley, roughly chopped
1 scallion, finely chopped
1 cup white beans, cooked
1 can solid white tuna, drained and flaked
1 copy Cassell's English~Surfer/Surfer~English dictionary

Chew on This

Eating pasta is said to cause the brain to produce seratonin, a natural substance that helps bring about calmness and a sense of well-being. Next time you're feeling bogus, fill up a bowl and go party, dude.

INSIDE SCOOP

The scene where Jeff Spicoli explains world history to Mr. Hand is the supposed inspiration for *Bill & Ted's Excellent Adventure.*

- **Make the dressing:** In a small mixing bowl, combine the olive oil, red pepper, lemon juice, garlic, dill, and salt. Whisk together, cover, and refrigerate.
- **Prepare the pasta:** Cook the pasta al dente (a little less than package instructions may call for). Drain, rinse well 2 or 3 times, and toss with a little olive oil.
- **Make the salad:** In a large mixing bowl, combine the pasta and the rest of the salad ingredients and toss together. Whisk the dressing once more, pour over the salad, and toss a few times to mix evenly. Yield: 6–8 servings.
- If you plan to eat this dish in history class, triple the recipe. That way, when the teacher says, "Did you bring enough for everyone?" you can say you did.

1 Never let on how much you like her.

2 Call the shots.

3 Wherever you are, *that's* the place to be.

4 Order for the both of you.

5 When making out, put on Side One of *Led Zeppelin IV.*

—Damone's (Robert Romanus) Never-Fail 5 Points for Success with Chicks

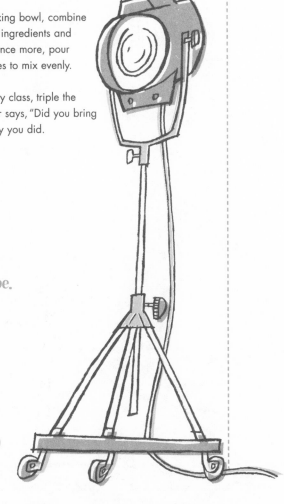

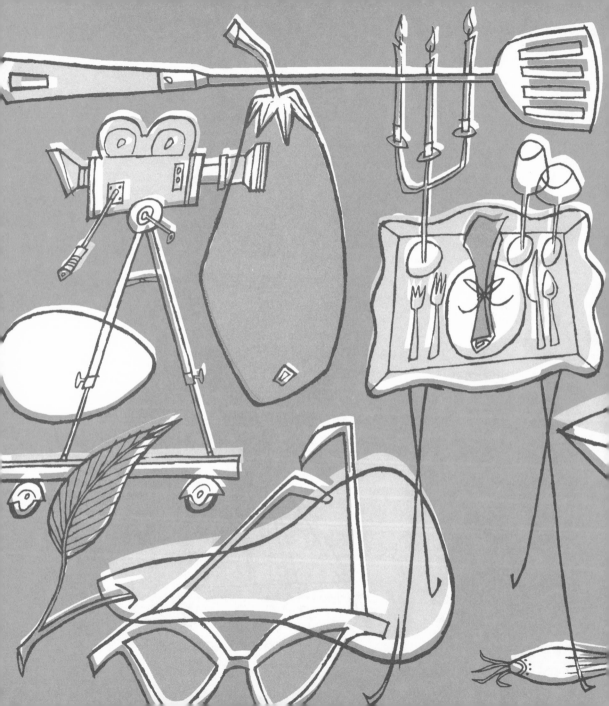

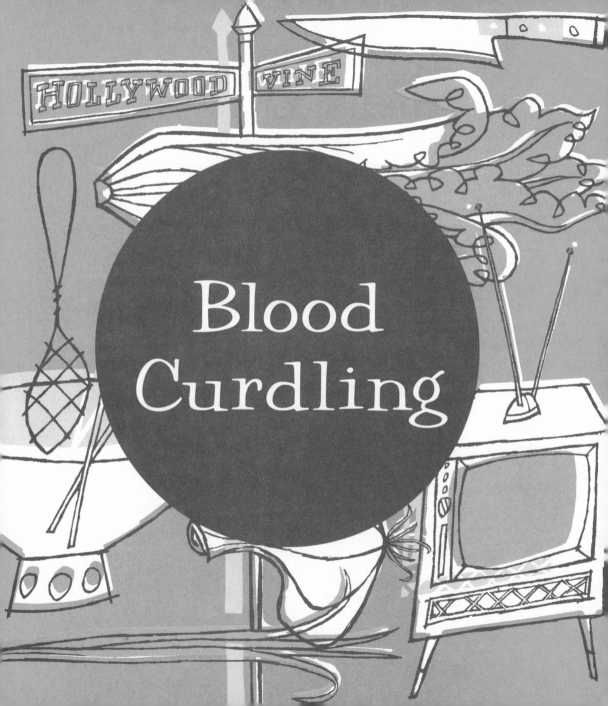

Blood Curdling

Steak-Through-the-Heart Tartar

(Attention: This recipe contains an important warning.)

Here's something to really sink your vampire fangs into. Though not for the faint of heart, when this dish is prepared properly, your guests will be eternally grateful. Remember, never confuse the Uncooked with the Undead.

For the Roasted Garlic
6 whole heads garlic, unpeeled
3 Tbsp extra virgin olive oil, divided
½ tsp kosher salt
½ tsp freshly ground black pepper
5 sprigs fresh thyme
½ baguette, thinly sliced

For the Steak-Through-the-Heart Tartar
1 cup brandy or cognac
1½ lbs very fresh sirloin steak, trimmed
½ tsp Worcestershire sauce
1 Tbsp Dijon mustard
Kosher salt
Freshly ground black pepper
1 egg yolk

For the Garnishes
4 Tbsp finely chopped parsley
4 Tbsp finely chopped red onion
4 Tbsp capers
4 Tbsp finely chopped shallots
1 Tbsp extra virgin olive oil
1 dash cayenne pepper
1 set wax fangs

Food for Thought

GARLIC TIP
#44
It has been said that garlic first sprouted in the Garden of Eden in the footprints of Lucifer.

WARNING: Although many dishes using raw meat are enjoyed throughout the world, the USDA strongly advises against anyone ever eating raw meat. This especially applies to children, the elderly, and anyone with health concerns.

- Preheat oven to 325°F. In a baking dish or pie plate, toss the garlic with salt, pepper, thyme, and 1 tablespoon of the olive oil. Cover loosely with foil and roast for 45 minutes, until soft and golden.
- Brush the baguette slices with the other 2 tablespoons of olive oil, place on a cookie sheet, and bake with garlic for the last 15 minutes of cooking.
- While the garlic is roasting, assemble the ingredients needed for the tartar. If using a food processor, wash the blade and bowl assembly well and place in the freezer. Remove meat from refrigerator, rinse well with cold water, and blot dry with a paper towel. On a clean cutting board, trim and discard ⅛-inch all around the outer edge of the steak.
- Place the trimmed meat in a small dish, cover with brandy, and refrigerate 10 minutes. Pour off and discard brandy and cut the meat into 1-inch cubes. Transfer half to the chilled food processor and pulse a few times until meat is coarsely chopped. Repeat with the second half. Cover with plastic wrap and return to the refrigerator for 10 minutes.
- In a medium mixing bowl, combine the chopped sirloin with the Worcestershire and Dijon mustard. Season with salt and freshly ground pepper to taste.
- On a chilled platter, form meat into the shape of a plump heart. Make an indentation in the center of the heart and fill with the whole egg yolk. Surround the heart with a coffin-shaped border of parsley and onion, plus little caper bats and shallot full moons. Drizzle a little olive oil over the top of the meat and dust with cayenne.
- Remove garlic and bread from oven. Slice off the tops of the garlic and immediately suck them dry . . . or arrange artfully on the platter alongside the succulent, bloodred heart of life-giving meat that seems to be calling to you.
- Serve immediately to your waiting victims or guests. Yield: 4 servings.

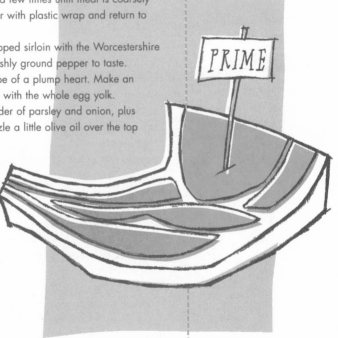

Chew on This

How to spot a vampire: if their driver's license says they are more than 2,000 years old and they have no picture.

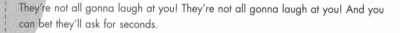

Carrie's Prom Crisp

They're not all gonna laugh at you! They're not all gonna laugh at you! And you can bet they'll ask for seconds.

For the Fruit Filling
5–6 Fuji or Granny Smith apples (about 6 cups when sliced)
2 Tbsp fresh lemon juice
1½ pints strawberries, hulled and quartered
2–3 Tbsp sugar, depending on sweetness of the fruit
1 Tbsp all-purpose flour
1 tsp vanilla

For the Crisp Topping
1 cup walnuts
1 cup all-purpose flour
½ cup light brown sugar
2 Tbsp white sugar
⅓ cup oatmeal
1½ tsp cinnamon
½ cup cold butter, cut into ¼-inch pieces
15 gallons pig blood, well aged

- Sit perfectly still in a comfortable chair. Using only the untapped power of your impassioned epicurean mind, *will* the razor-sharp knife to peel, core, and thinly slice the fleshy fruit of the apples in a macabre dance of flashing steel and flying peel. Preheat the oven to 350°F and grease a 10- to 12-inch cast-iron skillet with butter.
- **For the Filling:** Toss fruit slices with lemon juice to prevent darkening. In a large mixing bowl, combine the vanilla, sugars, and flour. Add the apples and strawberries and toss gently to mix, being careful not to break apart the apple slices.

Chew on This

Fruit crisps are easy to make and hard to ruin. Although we used apples and strawberries, try experimenting with seasonal fruits and other types of nuts.

- **For the Crisp Topping:** Lay walnut pieces on a cookie sheet and toast for 10 minutes in the 350°F oven. Cool and chop viciously into small pieces.
- In a medium mixing bowl combine the flour, sugars, oatmeal, and cinnamon. Add the walnuts and stir together. Work the butter pieces into the topping mixture a little at a time with your fingers or a pastry blender. Continue blending until the topping holds together and crumbles to the size of small peas.
- **Assembly:** Pour the fruit filling evenly into the buttered skillet. Distribute the topping over the filling, pressing down lightly.
- **Fire Drill:** Put the skillet in the hot oven. Slam and lock the oven door. Walk slowly out into the night. (Make sure to return in 40–45 minutes to find the topping brown and crunchy and the glistening crimson juices beginning to bubble up and ooze from the surface.) Eat without mercy.

Yield: 6–8 servings.

INSIDE SCOOP

Carrie Fisher was originally set to play the lead role in *Carrie*, but she refused to do the nude scenes. She eventually switched roles with Sissy Spacek, who had been cast in a film, then in development, called *Star Wars*.

Big-Foot-Long Hot Dogs

There were times after beginning our search for the elusive "healthful-yet-tasty hot dog" when we felt we had a better chance of finding Sasquatch at a swap meet. It seems we underestimated ourselves. This very low-fat, all-chicken foot-long is loaded with flavor, while the only Yeti sightings we've witnessed so far have been in this 1987 comedy starring John Lithgow (although a friend of ours thought he saw a Chupacabra near a car wash once).

¾ lb chicken thigh meat, skinless and boneless
¾ lb chicken breast meat, skinless and boneless
1 tsp soy sauce
1 tsp minced garlic
1 egg white
½ tsp onion powder
2 tsp paprika
1½ tsp salt
¼ tsp celery seed
¼ tsp ground sage
½ tsp white pepper
1½ tsp sugar
1 cup ice cubes
1 very large flea comb

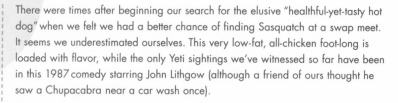

Chew on This

John Lithgow has been nominated for an Academy Award® for Best Supporting Actor twice–for *The World According to Garp* and *Terms of Endearment.*

Food for Thought

The hot dog was given its current name in 1901. Until that time, the product had been sold under the name "red-hot dachshund sausages." (Perhaps someone had trouble spelling dachshund.)

- Cut up the chicken in ½-inch pieces and place in a medium mixing bowl. Add and stir in the soy sauce, garlic, and egg white. In a small bowl, combine the onion powder, paprika, salt, celery seed, sage, white pepper, and sugar. Pour the spice mixture over the chicken and mix in well. Place the bowl in the freezer and chill for 30 minutes.
- Put the ice cubes in the bowl of a food processor fitted with a metal cutting blade. Process for 30 seconds until well pulverized; scrape the ice into a bowl and set aside. Add the chicken to the processor bowl and grind in 2 15-second

pulses, scraping the sides of the bowl with a rubber spatula between pulses. Add the crushed ice and grind for a final 20 seconds.

- Transfer the ground chicken to a pastry bag with a ¾-inch opening. Oil a 15-inch length of aluminum foil and pipe out 6 nice big-foot longs side by side. Bring 1 inch of water to a boil in a large skillet or saucepan; carefully transfer the foil and the footlongs into the pan. Cover and reduce the heat to medium. Steam for 8–10 minutes. Remove the dogs and either serve hot from the pan with garnishes of choice or plunge in ice water to cool quickly before wrapping and refrigerating. Yield: 6 big-foot-longs.

Chew on This

This movie won an Academy Award for Best Makeup.

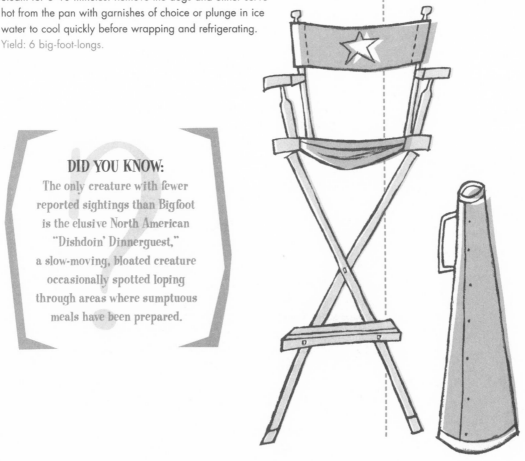

DID YOU KNOW:
The only creature with fewer reported sightings than Bigfoot is the elusive North American "Dishdoin' Dinnerguest," a slow-moving, bloated creature occasionally spotted loping through areas where sumptuous meals have been prepared.

It-Was-Alive! Calamari with Aioli

They called us mad when we said we could create the perfect snack. Harnessing all the powers of modern food science, we've brought this monstrously satisfying creation to life.

For the Aioli
2 egg yolks
4 garlic cloves, minced
½ tsp Dijon mustard
½ tsp salt
⅛ tsp cayenne pepper
1 tsp red wine vinegar
1 cup pure olive oil
2 Tbsp lemon juice
1 Tbsp ice water, as needed
1 Tbsp Italian parsley, chopped

For the Calamari
2 lbs squid, cleaned
2 cups bread crumbs
1 Tbsp fresh oregano or marjoram, chopped
2 eggs, mixed with ⅓ cup cold water
2 cups all-purpose flour
Canola oil, for frying
3 lemons, cut into wedges
100 frightened and angry townspeople with torches and miscellaneous farm tools
1 beaker raging teenage hormones

- **Create the aioli:** Place bra or other stretchy female garment on head; proceed to next step.
- Rinse mixing bowl with warm water and dry thoroughly.

INSIDE SCOOP

When cooking squid, keep in mind something that many chefs refer to as the "2/20 Rule." If squid cooks much longer than 2 minutes it will get very tough. But if this happens, don't panic. Turn down the heat and continue cooking for 20 minutes until it becomes tender again.

- Place egg yolks in mixing bowl and whisk till smooth and creamy. Throw head back and laugh like mad scientist. Add the garlic, mustard, salt, cayenne pepper, and vinegar and continue whisking feverishly.
- Continue whisking as though madly possessed by your new abilities to create life, adding half the olive oil very slowly. (The mixture should begin to grow and emulsify.) After half the oil has been used, add the lemon juice; then whisk in the remaining oil. If the mixture seems a little too thick, whisk in a splash of ice water; if too thin, whisk in a little more olive oil.
- Add the parsley; taste and adjust seasonings as desired; cover and refrigerate.
- Create the calamari: Wrestle the squid into the work area (or just pull the package from the fridge). Slice into ¼- to ½-inch rings. (If the tentacles are large, cut them in half lengthwise first.) Rinse with cold water and dry very well with paper towels or in a salad spinner.
- Heat 4 inches of oil in a heavy saucepan or fryer to 340°–350°F.
- Mix together the bread crumbs and oregano. Dust a handful of squid lightly with flour, shaking off the excess in a strainer; dip in the egg wash and dredge in the bread crumbs. (If you prefer a lighter coating on the calamari, omit the egg wash and bread crumbs and fry with just the flour coating.)
- Frying in batches, add the calamari to the hot oil. Cook for 2 minutes, until golden, and drain on paper towels. Repeat until all the squid is cooked. Serve hot with a squeeze of lemon and the aioli. Yield: 4 servings.
- After you've completed this experiment, roll up the sleeves on your stained and splattered lab coat and bask in the glory of your creations. Will everyone finally realize what a great culinary genius you really are? (Or will they still make you do the dishes?)

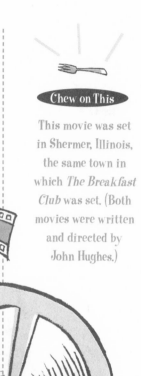

Chew on This

This movie was set in Shermer, Illinois, the same town in which *The Breakfast Club* was set. (Both movies were written and directed by John Hughes.)

Seasonings
Greetings

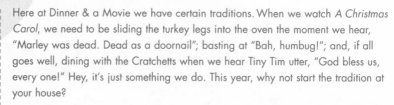

Scrooge's Turkey Legs with Crispy Gruel Stuffing

Here at Dinner & a Movie we have certain traditions. When we watch *A Christmas Carol*, we need to be sliding the turkey legs into the oven the moment we hear, "Marley was dead. Dead as a doornail"; basting at "Bah, humbug!"; and, if all goes well, dining with the Cratchetts when we hear Tiny Tim utter, "God bless us, every one!" Hey, it's just something we do. This year, why not start the tradition at your house?

Chew on This

Although our recipe calls for drumsticks, most turkeys are raised for maximum production of white meat. It's not uncommon for their breasts to get so big that they can't get near enough to each other to mate.

For Scrooge's Turkey Legs

3 large onions, peeled and sliced
   in ½-inch rings
1 Tbsp minced garlic
4 Tbsp olive oil
6 turkey drumsticks, on sale if possible
Salt and pepper
1 set of chains, forged in life,
   to be worn eternally

For the Crispy Gruel Stuffing

¼ cup dry vermouth
½ cup golden raisins
8 oz pork sausage
1 onion, chopped
1 cup chopped celery
2 Granny Smith apples, peeled,
   cored, and chopped
1½ cups gruel (dry oatmeal)
3 cups dried bread cubes
1 cup walnut pieces
½ cup chicken broth
1 egg, beaten
1 tsp ground sage
¼ cup chopped fresh parsley
½ tsp freshly ground black pepper
2 oz (½ stick) melted butter

- **Roast the legs:** Preheat oven to 350°F. Brush the onion slices with a little olive oil and lay side by side in a shallow roasting pan. Combine the garlic with the remaining olive oil and rub onto the drumsticks. Season with salt and pepper.

- Arrange the turkey legs over the onion slices and place pan in the lower third of the preheated oven. Roast for a total of 90 minutes. (The stuffing goes in the oven for the last 45 minutes of cooking.) Occasionally baste both the stuffing and the legs with any accumulated pan juices.
- **Make the stuffing:** Put the golden raisins in a small saucepan, cover with vermouth, and bring to a simmer. Remove from heat and set aside.
- In a large skillet over medium heat, lightly brown the sausage, breaking it up as it cooks. Use a slotted spoon to transfer sausage to a large mixing bowl and set aside. Add the onion and celery to the skillet and cook until softened. Stir in the chopped apples and cook 15 minutes, stirring often. Add the raisins and vermouth, increase the heat to high, and cook until most of the liquid has evaporated. Scrape the hot mixture into the mixing bowl containing the sausage, stir together, and cool to room temperature.
- Fold in 1 cup oatmeal, 2 cups bread cubes, ½ cup walnuts, chicken broth, and the beaten egg. Season with sage, parsley, and black pepper and mix together well. Turn the mixture into a well-buttered shallow casserole or baking dish, sprinkle the remaining gruel, bread cubes, and walnuts evenly over the top and drizzle with melted butter.
- On a single dinner plate, balance all six turkey legs atop the pile of now caramelized onions, surrounded by a ring of crispy gruel stuffing. *Eat every bite yourself.* Don your nightcap, climb into bed, and see which shows up first: the ghost of Christmas Past or the pain of heartburn present.

Yield: 4–6 servings (or 1 miser).

Food for Thought

"I have endeavoured in this ghostly little book, to raise the ghost of an idea, which shall not put my readers out of humour with themselves, with each other, with the season, or with me. May it haunt their houses pleasantly."

—Charles Dickens, December 1843

Standing Rib Roast with Rockshire Pudding

It was the best of times, it was the worst of times, it was the beginning of time, it was the Stone Age. If you've ever been afraid to make a standing rib roast, don't be. This recipe is easy to yabba-dabba-do.

Chew on This

ROAST TIP
#45

Don't ask the butcher to remove the bones on your roast. They keep the roast moist and help conduct heat evenly, allowing the meat to cook in less time.

For the Standing Rib Roast
6 lbs prime rib (2–3 ribs,
　ask for "first cut")
1 Tbsp kosher salt
1 Tbsp freshly ground black pepper
2 Tbsp olive oil

For the Rockshire Pudding
2 eggs
1 tsp salt
1 pinch nutmeg
¼ tsp minced fresh thyme
1 cup milk
1 cup all-purpose flour
3 Tbsp ice water
3 Tbsp fat (rendered from the roast)

For the Vegetables
½ lb brussels sprouts, trimmed
½ lb small white onions, whole, peeled
1 lb small red potatoes, cut in half
1 stocking-full quarry rocks,
　freshly cracked

For the Horseradish Sauce
4 Tbsp freshly grated horseradish,
　mixed with 2 Tbsp white-wine
　vinegar, or 4 Tbsp prepared
　horseradish
1 cup sour cream
¼ tsp white pepper
½ tsp salt
1 tsp sugar

- **Prepare the rib roast:** After you've discovered fire, adjust rack to the lower third of the oven and preheat oven to 450°F. Rinse and dry meat. In a small bowl, combine the salt, pepper, and olive oil. Rub oil into roast, and arrange fat side up in a shallow roasting pan. Place in the preheated oven and roast for 20 minutes.
- Reduce oven temperature to 325°F. Continue roasting for another hour, or until a meat thermometer inserted in the larger end of the roast reads about 120°F

for rare, 130°F for medium rare, or 140°F for medium. (If not using a meat thermometer, calculate 13–18 minutes total cooking time per pound of meat.)

- **Prepare the veggies:** Add the prepared vegetables to the roasting pan during the last 45 minutes of cooking.
- **Prepare the Rockshire pudding:** Combine the eggs, salt, nutmeg, and thyme; beat until fluffy. Alternately add the milk and flour and continue beating until smooth. Refrigerate until use.
- **Prepare the horseradish sauce:** Squeeze excess vinegar from the grated horseradish (omit this step if using prepared horseradish). Combine with remaining ingredients and whisk until creamy. Set aside for flavors to blend.
- Remove the roast to a platter and allow to rest at room temperature for 30 minutes before carving. This allows the roast to finish cooking evenly and gives the juices time to be reabsorbed into the meat. While the roast rests, raise the oven temperature to 400°F for the Rockshire pudding.
- Heat rendered fat from the roasting pan in a large cast-iron skillet over medium-high heat until it begins to sizzle. Whisk ice water into the batter and pour all at once into the hot skillet. Bake in the 400°F oven until puffy, crisp, and golden brown. Cool and cut into wedges. Yield: 4 servings. (Save leftovers for roast-beast sandwiches.)
- Gather the clan (make sure you've invited guests who have opposable thumbs), pull up your favorite rock, and give thanks for this truly prehistoric occasion.

Food for Thought

If Dickens had been alive in the Stone Age, would he have been known as Charles Dickrock?

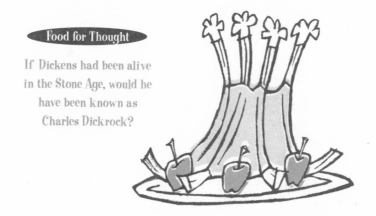

Few people know that this masterful epic almost didn't made it to the big screen. According to *The Hollyrock Reporter*, it was rumored that during the filming of this movie, Fred and Wilma had creative differences. This was due to the fact that Wilma was weary of the network television grind and wanted to return to her first love, the theater, but Fred wanted to break into feature films. He felt he was being typecast as a big Stone Age guy. At one point, Fred's confidence was so shattered he had trouble remembering his dialogue. "Yabba-da . . . Line, please?" The production was halted for three days while the lawyers hammered out a compromise. Luckily for us they did. The work speaks for itself.

"Edible" Fruitcake ... No, Really

Hey, hey, hey, wait a minute, before you turn that page . . . You should know that this fruitcake has been designed to be less dense than the traditional, family heirloom, brandy-soaked, half-life of plutonium, door-stopper kind of fruit cake. It actually can be enjoyed warm out of the oven if desired.

For the "Fruit-" Part
1½ cups dried, diced apricots (½-inch chunks)
1½ cups dried cranberries
1½ cups golden raisins
1 cup diced pineapple (½-inch chunks)
¼ cup Gran Marnier
1 cup coarsely chopped pecans
1 cup coarsely chopped blanched almonds

For the "-cake" Part
2 sticks butter, softened
½ cup light brown sugar
1 cup confectioner's sugar
Zest of 1 lemon, grated
Zest of 2 oranges or tangerines, grated
6 eggs, separated
2 tsp vanilla extract
½ tsp almond extract
2½ cups all-purpose flour
½ tsp salt
1 tsp baking powder
2 tsp ground cinnamon
½ tsp ground nutmeg
¼ tsp ground ginger
1 leg of lamp

Chew on This

Harper's Index once listed the density of the average fruitcake as being the same as that of mahogany.

Food for Thought

Want to turn your next ill-advised winter pole-licking dare into a party? **Try our version:** the refreshing "Fruity Frozen Flagpole."© Just pour your favorite fruit juice on a frozen outdoor pole and watch the fun. We feel that since your tongue will be painfully stuck to the pole for a long while, it should at least taste good. Your guests will never want to leave! . . . Well, they can't.

- Preheat oven to 250°F. Butter 2 9 x 5-inch loaf pans and line with parchment paper or aluminum foil. Butter the paper or foil and set aside.
- In a medium mixing bowl, combine the apricots, cranberries, golden raisins, pineapple, and Gran Marnier; stir well and set aside. In another mixing bowl, sift together the flour, salt, baking powder, cinnamon, nutmeg, and ginger. Add the chopped nuts and toss a few times.
- In a large mixing bowl, cream together the brown sugar, confectioner's sugar, and butter until fluffy and smooth. Blend in the egg yolks, one at a time, allowing each to incorporate before adding the next. Stir in the vanilla, almond extract, lemon zest, and orange zest.
- To the butter mixture, alternately fold in the flour mixture and the fruit mixture; stir until well blended. Beat the egg whites until soft peaks begin to form. A third at a time, fold the beaten egg whites into the batter.
- Pour half of the batter into each of the prepared pans, filling them no more than 1 inch from the top. Smooth out the tops and bake about 2 hours. To see if the fruitcake is cooked through, insert a knife or skewer in the center. If the knife emerges clean, you might as well put in all the rest of your silver and clean it while you've got the chance. Cool in the pans for 30 minutes, turn out, and brush the tops and sides with a little Gran Marnier. Eat warm, or wrap tightly in plastic wrap and refrigerate. Yield: 2 9 x 5-inch fruitcakes.
- Note: If what you want is a fruitcake that can withstand the ravages of time better than yourself, double the Gran Marnier and add at least two cups of brandy or rum to the dried fruit. Soak for 24 hours before proceeding with recipe. (The next thing to do is decide who in the family is worthy of inheriting these durable, fruity monoliths in years to come.)

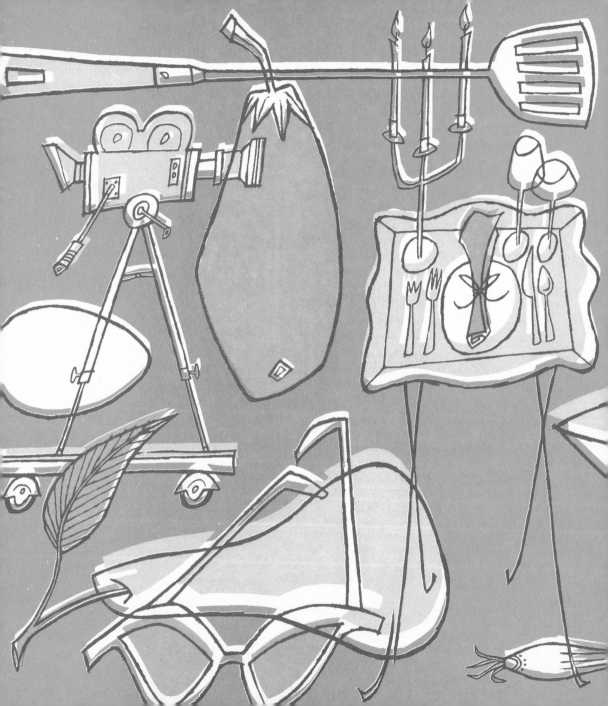

HOLLYWOOD VINE

Time
& Thyme
Again

Napoleon's "Bone-Apart" Snapper Sandwiches

Even though Napoleon is given credit for this sandwich, it was Bill and Ted who turned him on to the most excellent potato-chip crust. Cook on, dudes!

For the Bone-Apart Snapper
4 6-oz snapper filets, skinned, boned, and ready to party
½ cup heavy cream (half-and-half)
2 cups barbecued potato chips, finely ground (like dust in the wind, dude)
2 Tbsp peanut oil

4 excellent French rolls

For the Tartar Sauce
½ cup mayonnaise
1 tsp capers
3 Tbsp sweet pickles, diced
1 scallion, finely chopped
1 Tbsp freshly squeezed lemon juice
⅛ tsp freshly ground black pepper

For the Rest of the Tasty Toppings
1 cup very thinly sliced red onion
3 cups shredded iceberg lettuce
¼ cup roughly chopped fresh dill
2–3 Tbsp sliced, pickled jalapeño peppers, with juice
2 ripe tomatoes, sliced
1 exceptionally loud musical instrument of any type
   (no actual proficiency required)

INSIDE SCOOP

Scores of different fish are sold under the name red snapper. Most of them are mild, white-fleshed fish that wouldn't be easy to sell under their real names. (Bill & Ted's Blubberlip Sandwiches?)

- **Prep the filets, dude:** Preheat oven to 450°F. Rinse the snapper filets in cold water and blot dry with paper towels. Place in a bowl, cover with the cream, and refrigerate 10 minutes.
- Pour 1 cup of the ground potato chips into a shallow baking dish just large enough to accommodate the filets. Remove the snapper from the cream and lay side by side over the ground chips. Sprinkle the remaining potato chips evenly over the filets and cover with plastic wrap. Press the coating firmly into the fish with a spatula and refrigerate for 15 minutes, while making the tartar sauce.
- **Totally make the tartar sauce:** Combine the mayonnaise with the capers, sweet pickle, and scallion. Stir in the lemon juice and season with black pepper.
- **Look out for the iceberg, dude!** In a medium bowl, combine the lettuce, onion, dill, and jalapeños. Cover and refrigerate.
- **Get totally crispy:** On the stove, heat peanut oil in a large cast-iron skillet on medium-high heat. Place the coated filets in the hot pan and cook for 2 minutes, without turning. Transfer skillet to the hot oven and continue cooking, uncovered, for 8 minutes. Place the rolls in the oven, cut side up, to toast during the last 2 minutes of cooking time.
- **Time for munchies:** Pile copious amounts of tartar sauce, tomatoes, and spicy iceberg on each roll, top with the snapper, and chow down.
- **Gnarly Philosophical Tip:** Always remember, dudes, the most awesome way to be excellent to each other is through the righteous and timely preparation of totally succulent chow.
  Yield: 4 excellent servings.

Chew on This

Genghis Khan never ate off a plate at home like he does in this movie.

Predestined Cosmic Curry

This 1990 comedy deals with the issues of fate and chance. We see something in your future: It's steaming hot, highly seasoned, and—wait—it appears to be served over a bed of rice.

The Spices

1 Tbsp coriander seed
1 Tbsp cumin seed
½ tsp fennel seed
½ tsp black or yellow mustard seed
¼ tsp cardamom (optional)
¼ tsp fenugreek (optional)
½ tsp chili powder
1½ tsp ground turmeric
⅛ tsp ground cloves
¼ tsp cayenne pepper

The Rest

2–3 Tbsp clarified butter
1 yellow onion, thinly sliced
2 serrano or jalapeño chilis, seeded and thinly sliced
4 cloves garlic, thinly sliced

1 Tbsp fresh ginger, grated
2 carrots, peeled and cut into ½-inch slices
5 small red potatoes, cut into eighths
1 cup baby corn
1 cauliflower, cut in small florets
2 small zucchini, cut into ½-inch slices
3 ripe tomatoes, roughly chopped
1 12-oz can coconut milk
1 cup water or chicken stock
1 cup peas, fresh or frozen (if fresh, boil for 2 minutes)
1 Tbsp cider vinegar
Salt and pepper
1 friendly bartender with powers far beyond those of normal bartenders

INSIDE SCOOP

For maximum flavor at less cost, buy whole spices rather than ground spices. Grind them as needed in an old coffee grinder.

- In a small saucepan, over medium heat, dry roast the coriander, cumin, fennel, mustard seed, cardamom, and fenugreek for about 2 minutes, stirring and shaking the pan often. If the pan is hot enough, the spices should begin to pop and smoke a little.
- Transfer the toasted seeds to a mortar and pestle or spice grinder and pulverize. Combine with the remaining spices and set aside for later.

- Heat the butter in a large skillet and fry the onion and chili over medium heat, stirring often, until the onions are golden brown.
- Add the garlic and ginger and cook for another minute or two, then add the spice mixture and fry for a minute longer.
- Add the carrots, potatoes, baby corn, cauliflower, and zucchini and sauté for 5 minutes. Add a little more clarified butter if the pan seems too dry.
- Add the chopped tomatoes, coconut milk, and water or chicken stock and simmer, uncovered, for 30–45 minutes. Add a little more water or chicken stock as needed if the sauce gets too thick.
- Add the peas no more than 1 or 2 minutes prior to service. Season with a tablespoon of cider vinegar, and salt and pepper to taste. Serve with rice. Yield: 6 servings.
- Enjoy every bite as though it's your first, last, and only meal ever to be eaten in this, or any other existence. (Then slip away to a parallel universe and wait till the kitchen's been cleaned up.)

Did You Know?

Mr. Destiny's Rene Russo was one of the original "supermodels".

Food for Thought

Curry powder is not a spice. It's actually a specific blend of up to 15 spices.

Travelin' Through Thyme & Onion Tart

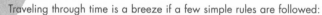

Traveling through time is a breeze if a few simple rules are followed:
1. Always reset your watch.
2. Never date your mom.
3. Never do anything that would cause you not to be born (see #2).
4. Never leave potato salad in a hot car.

For the Filling
1 medium white onion, thinly sliced
2 medium red onions, thinly sliced
2 Tbsp extra virgin olive oil
1 tsp light brown sugar
1 Tbsp fresh thyme, chopped
½ cup light-bodied red wine (Beaujolais is nice)
Salt and freshly ground black pepper

For the Tart Shell and Toppings
1 sheet frozen puff pastry dough (the most popular brand contains 2 10-inch sheets)
1 egg beaten with 1 Tbsp of cold water
½ cup grated Parmesan cheese
15 tasty black olives, pitted and chopped
1 6-oz jar artichoke hearts in water, drained and quartered
A little thyme on your hands

• **Time to make the filling:** Heat the olive oil and butter in a large skillet on medium heat. Add the onions and brown sugar; cook for 15 minutes, stirring often. Add the red wine and increase the heat to medium high. Continue cooking about 10 minutes, until the wine is reduced completely and the onions have the

Chew on This

When cutting onions, tearing is caused by 2 enzymes that, when combined, create that all-too-familiar eye irritation. Some tricks to lessen the effect include:

1 using the sharpest knife possible

2 refrigerating the onions before cutting

3 cutting directly under the range-top exhaust vent.

consistency of thick marmalade. Stir in the thyme and season to taste with salt and pepper. Set aside to cool.

- **Time to form the tart:** Place a large cookie sheet on a rack in the lower third of the oven and preheat oven to 425°F.
- Lay out the puff pastry sheet flat on a lightly floured surface. Gently roll out the dough to a 10-inch square, dusting with a little flour to avoid sticking. Transfer the dough to a well-buttered sheet of aluminum foil.
- Using a small pastry brush, paint a 1-inch border of the egg mixture around the perimeter of the pastry square. One at a time, fold over each egg-washed edge to create an inch-wide double thickness border around the tart; brush the egg mixture over the doubled edge. In the area inside the border, use the tines of a fork to lightly prick the dough at ½-inch intervals. This will prevent the bottom crust from puffing.
- **Time to fill:** Sprinkle ¼ cup of the Parmesan evenly over the inner square of the pastry base. Spread the cooled onion mixture over the Parmesan and scatter the artichoke hearts and olives on top.
- **Time to bake:** Carefully lift the tart by the edges of the foil and slide onto the hot cookie sheet. Bake for 30 minutes until puffy, crisp, and golden brown. Garnish with chopped thyme. Yield: 1 8-inch tart.

Thymely Tip: If you suddenly realize that you have erred in one step of this recipe and feel it absolutely necessary to travel back in time to correct it, don't get carried away and alter the course of gastronomic history. You just might return to find tonight's menu changed to corndogs and Jell-O. Bon Appétit!

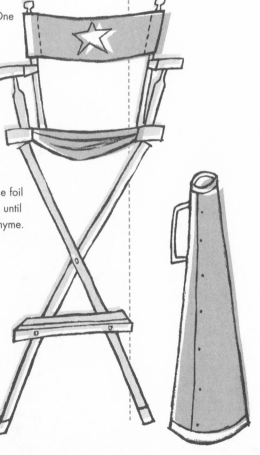

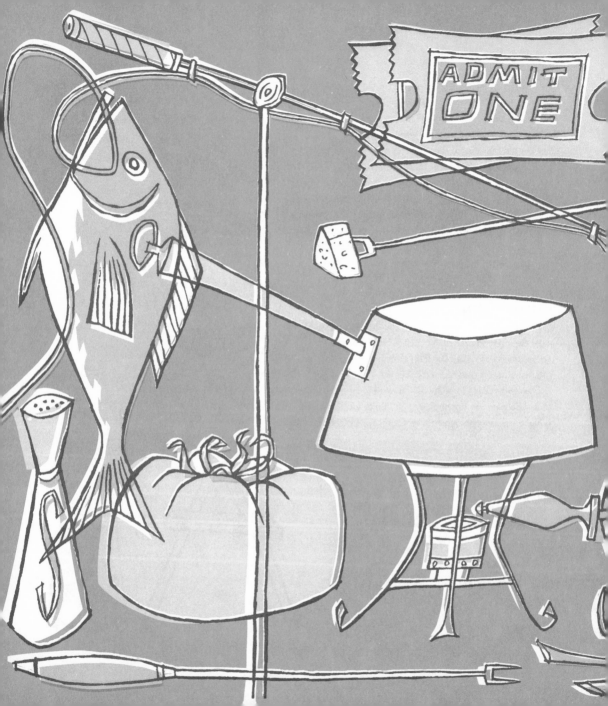

Shake Rattle & Rolls

Kevin Bacon & Cheese Hush Puppies

This movie reminds us of a story we once heard about a small Midwestern town where all dinner parties were outlawed after a tragic fondue accident. Kids were forced to smuggle trays of hors d'oeuvres across the county line. One day a mysterious stranger rode into town with nothing but a well-seasoned cast-iron skillet, a vision, and this recipe.

INSIDE SCOOP

In real life, Kevin Bacon's dancing body double (Peter Tramm) in *Footloose* was married to the dancing body double (Marine Jahan) for Jennifer Beals in *Flashdance*.

8 slices thick-cut bacon

For the Coating
1½ cups cornmeal
½ cup all-purpose flour
1 Tbsp sugar
1 Tbsp baking powder
½ tsp baking soda
½ cup grated cheddar cheese
1 tsp salt
1 tsp ground pepper

For the Breading
1 egg, beaten
½ tsp Tabasco sauce
1 cup buttermilk
4 scallions, minced
½ cup corn
3 Tbsp cold water, if needed

Corn oil for frying
¼ cup grated Parmesan cheese
1 empty factory with disco sound system and dance floor
1 angry and sensitive (but masculine) solo dance routine

- Cook the bacon until crisp. Cool and crumble into little bits.
- Stir together the following ingredients in a medium mixing bowl: cornmeal, flour, sugar, baking powder, baking soda, cheddar cheese, salt, and pepper. In a second bowl, mix together the beaten egg, Tabasco, buttermilk, scallions, bacon, and corn.
- Heat 2 inches of oil in a heavy saucepan over medium-high heat.

- Pour the egg mixture into the cornmeal mixture all at once and stir to make a very thick batter. (Add the cold water only if the batter seems too thick.)
- Scoop out rounded spoonfuls of batter and drop into the hot oil. (Don't overcrowd; they need room to dance.) Fry until golden brown, about 1 minute on each side. Roll the hot hush puppies in grated Parmesan cheese and listen to the howls of delight. Yield: 2 dozen pups.

Remember, when hush puppies are outlawed, only outlaws will have hush puppies (and you'll have to cross the state line to get 'em).

Chew on This

Try using a shoehorn to remove kernels from an ear of corn. (May we suggest washing it off first?)

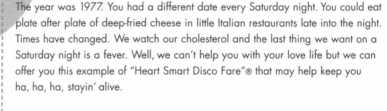

Tony Manero's "Stayin' Alive" Mozzarella Marinara

The year was 1977. You had a different date every Saturday night. You could eat plate after plate of deep-fried cheese in little Italian restaurants late into the night. Times have changed. We watch our cholesterol and the last thing we want on a Saturday night is a fever. Well, we can't help you with your love life but we can offer you this example of "Heart Smart Disco Fare"® that may help keep you ha, ha, ha, stayin' alive.

For the Marinara
1 28-oz can Italian plum tomatoes, cut in quarters
2 Tbsp extra virgin olive oil
3 anchovy filets, chopped
2 cloves garlic, peeled and thinly sliced
Chopped parsley
Freshly ground black pepper

For the Mozzarella
6 sheets frozen filo dough (also spelled phyllo and fillo), defrosted
3 Tbsp extra virgin olive oil
12 1-oz packages part-skim mozzarella (also labeled string cheese)
1 cup bread crumbs
¼ cup finely shredded fresh basil
Whole fresh basil leaves for garnish

• **Prepare for a hot night:** Preheat oven to 325°F. In a large mixing bowl, combine and toss together the tomatoes, olive oil, anchovies, and garlic. Spread out the contents of the bowl on a large cookie sheet and roast for 30 minutes, stirring once or twice. Transfer to the work bowl of a food processor or blender and give no more than 3–4 short pulses. The sauce should still be somewhat

Chew on This

The soundtrack to *Saturday Night Fever*, along with that of *Grease*, is in the list of top 5 grossing soundtracks of all time.

chunky. Season with chopped parsley and fresh ground black pepper to taste. Cover and keep in a warm spot.

- **Dress up the mozzarella:** Increase the oven temperature to 375°F. Lay out 1 piece of filo on a clean, dry surface. (Keep the remaining pieces covered with a damp cloth until use or they will dry out and crack.) Cut 2 strips, 6–7 inches wide from the first sheet. Lay the strips side by side and brush both sides of each strip lightly with olive oil.

- Sprinkle 1 tablespoon of bread crumbs and ½ teaspoon of basil evenly over the top of each strip. Center 1 piece of cheese at the end of the filo strip closest to you and roll up tightly. The filo-wrapped cheese should resemble a small cigar. Fold the ends under, sprinkle with bread crumbs, and place on an ungreased baking sheet. Repeat process for each piece of the remaining cheese. Bake for 10 minutes until cigars are hot and crispy.

- **Strut your stuff:** Lay out 6 warmed plates and make a pool of marinara in the center of each. Place 2 mozzarella cigars over the sauce and garnish with a basil leaf. Yield: 6 servings.

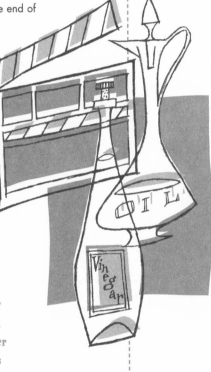

Food for Thought

Elvis died the year *Saturday Night Fever* was released.

Olive Oil Fact
#57

Olive oil is made up of nearly 75 percent monounsaturated fat, the type of fat that actually helps to lower high cholesterol levels in the body. It also contains elements believed to prevent cancer and slow the aging process. Some say it also aids in the ability to learn complex dance routines.

No Bull Tequila Fajitas

Originally, this recipe called for mechanical bull, but, not suprisingly, our butcher got electrocuted when he tried to bone out the loin. We use only chicken and shrimp in this mouthwatering, "bull free" creation.

For the Marinade
3 Roma tomatoes, cut in quarters
½ cup roughly chopped cilantro
½ yellow onion, roughly chopped
8 cloves garlic, peeled
½ cup beer (ah, leftovers you can love)
¼ cup tequila
¼ cup lime juice
3 Tbsp olive oil
2 tsp canned chipotle pepper

For the No Bull Fajitas
1 lb skinless, boneless chicken breasts
1 lb tiger shrimp
1 red onion, thinly sliced
2 pasilla peppers, seeded and
   thinly sliced
8–12 flour tortillas

For the Salsa
1 lb tomatillos, husks removed
4 cloves garlic, peeled
2 serrano peppers, peeled and seeded
½ cup chopped cilantro
½ tsp ground cumin
¼ tsp salt

For the Garnishes
3 ripe Roma tomatoes, diced
1 avocado, peeled, seeded, and sliced
1 cup sour cream
1 4-oz can pickled jalapeños
½ cup Jack or dry Mexican cheese,
   crumbled
1 cup shredded red cabbage
1 tsp oregano
1 "Don't Mess with Texas" T-shirt
1 subscription to *Mobile Home LIVING*
   magazine

Food for Thought

A general rule of thumb: the smaller the chile pepper, the hotter it is.

• **Move #1:** Place all ingredients for the marinade in a food processor or blender and blend until smooth. Clean and shell the shrimp, and cut the chicken breasts in strips. Place shrimp and chicken in separate nonreactive bowls, and add half of the marinade to each. Cover and refrigerate.

- **Move #2:** Heat a dry griddle or cast-iron skillet on medium-high heat. Place the tomatillos, garlic, and serranos on the griddle and roast for about 10 minutes until the tomatillo skins are blistered and dark brown. Transfer to a blender or food processor and blend for no more than 10 seconds (should be chunky). Transfer to a bowl and stir in the cilantro, cumin, and salt. Set aside for flavors to blend.
- **Time to really move it, pardner:** While the griddle is heating up, open a couple of Lone Stars and clean up the trailer. Shred the cabbage and toss with oregano and a little juice from the pickled jalapeños. Warm the tortillas. Clean and reheat the griddle on high heat.
- When the griddle is ready, grab a handful each of the chicken and the shrimp, squeeze out any excess marinade and toss onto the hot surface along with some red onion and pasilla pepper. If the griddle is hot enough, you're in for about a 2-minute ride.
- **Move it out:** Wrap meat in a warm tortilla; add sauce and garnishes to each plate. Hold on tight and don't let go.

Yield: 4 servings.

Tip: **We've found that this dish tastes better if any chewing tobacco is removed from mouth before consumption.**

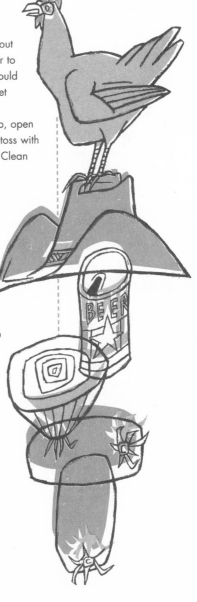

Chew on This

If you take the first 20 minutes of *Urban Cowboy* and make Travolta female, you'll have *Flashdance* (see page 74).

"Pink Lady" Pizza

Pizza is the word, is the word, is the word. It's got sauce, it's got feeling.

For the Dough
1 Tbsp active dry yeast
1 Tbsp honey
¼ cup cornmeal
¾ cup lukewarm water
½ tsp salt
3 Tbsp olive oil
2 cups all-purpose flour

For the Pink Lady Béchamel
1¾ cups milk, scalded
2 Tbsp butter
8 cloves garlic, thinly sliced
3 Tbsp all-purpose flour
1½ Tbsp tomato paste
1 Tbsp chopped fresh basil
¼ tsp salt
⅛ tsp white pepper

For the Toppings
¼ lb assorted wild mushrooms (such as portobello, shiitake, or morel), thinly sliced
¼ lb asparagus tips, sliced in half lengthwise
1 medium red onion, thinly sliced
2 cups smoked mozzarella, grated
1 telephone (to call for delivery when you come to your senses and realize
   that time spent in the kitchen equals time not spent on the dance floor)

- **Make the dough:** In a large mixing bowl, combine the yeast, honey,
  cornmeal, and ¼ cup of the water. Mix well and set aside to allow the yeast

Food for Thought

We don't want to say those kids look too old for high school, but word has it that half the girls were sent to the nurse's office for hot flashes.

to act (mixture should begin to foam and grow). After 15 minutes, add the remaining water, salt, and olive oil; mix well with a wooden spoon. Add 1½ cups of the flour and continue mixing until the ingredients form a cohesive mass.

- Transfer the dough onto a lightly floured surface and gradually knead in the remaining flour to create a soft, elastic dough. Continue kneading for 5–10 minutes (depending on how hungry you and your guests are), adding flour only to keep the dough from sticking, as needed.

- Transfer dough to a bowl oiled with a few drops of olive oil, turning to coat all sides of the dough evenly. Cover the bowl with a clean kitchen towel or plastic wrap and set in a warm, draft-free spot until doubled in size, 30–45 minutes.

- **Make the Pink Lady béchamel:** While the dough rises, bring the milk to a simmer over low heat in a small saucepan. In a medium, thick-bottomed saucepan, melt the butter over medium heat. To the butter add the garlic and flour and cook, without browning, for 2–3 minutes, stirring constantly with a wooden spoon. Add the tomato paste to the butter mixture, cook another minute, and reduce the heat to a low simmer. Whisk in the hot milk and simmer for 15 minutes, occasionally stirring and scraping the sides and bottom with a wooden spoon. Remove the sauce from heat, add the basil, and season with salt and pepper. Set aside to cool some.

- **It's the one that you want, ooh-ooh-ooh:** Preheat the oven to 550°F. Divide the dough in half, and roll and stretch each piece to a diameter of 10–14 inches. (A smaller diameter will produce a thicker, breadlike crust, while a larger diameter will yield a thinner, crispier crust.) Transfer the unbaked crusts to two floured pizza pans or a large cookie sheet.

- Spread each crust with a thin layer of béchamel sauce. Arrange the mushrooms, asparagus, and onion over the sauce and top with cheese. Slide the pan onto the oven floor (or on the lowest rack) and bake for 10 minutes, or until brown and bubbly. Yield: 2 medium pizza pies.

- Regardless of your actual age, feel free anytime to break into an off-the-cuff, boisterous song-and-dance routine. Muster all the innocent, teenage exuberance you possibly can.

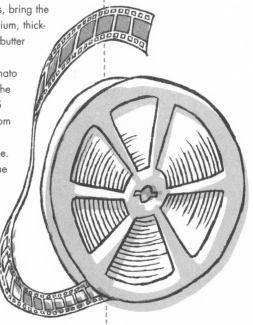

INSIDE SCOOP

The precursor to the modern-day pizza was made with a crust of crushed garbanzo beans.

I Want Liver Forever
(I wanna learn how to fry)

LOCATION: The Streets of New York City

FADE IN: Groups of promising young cooking students wildly dancing through the streets with whisks, paring knifes, and slotted spoons. Two have leapt onto a taxi cab and are air-sautéeing. . . . CUT TO:

For the Marinade and Liver
1½ lbs calves' liver, sliced ¼-inch thick, or as thinly as possible
2 cups cold milk
2 Tbsp finely chopped shallots
5 Tbsp extra virgin olive oil
4 Tbsp balsamic or sherry vinegar
1 Tbsp Dijon mustard

For the Flour Mixture
½ cup all-purpose flour
¾ cup bread crumbs
½ tsp salt
¼ tsp freshly ground black pepper

For the Sauce
Pure olive oil for sautéeing
3 Tbsp capers
1 Tbsp chopped shallots
¼ cup balsamic or sherry vinegar
1 cup beef stock
3 Tbsp cold butter, cut into pieces
2 Tbsp minced fresh parsley
1 subsciption to *Daily Variety Meats*

INSIDE SCOOP

When buying liver, choose lighter-colored calves' liver over beef liver whenever possible. Calves' liver is milder and more tender and doesn't have the bitterness often associated with mature beef liver.

DID YOU KNOW?

The title song won an Academy Award for Best Original Score and Best Original Song.

- **The liver prepares:** Rinse the liver well in cold water; place in a bowl and cover with cold milk while assembling the next few ingredients.
- In a small mixing bowl, combine the shallots, olive oil, and vinegar. Drain the milk well from the liver and stir in the shallot marinade. Cover and refrigerate for 20 minutes.
- Combine the flour, bread crumbs, and salt and pepper on a large plate and stir together with a fork.
- **Learn how to fry:** Heat a large frying pan over high heat with just enough oil to cover the bottom of the skillet. When the oil is very hot, dredge pieces of liver in the flour mixture and shake off the excess. Fry for no more than a minute on each side. The liver should be crisp and golden brown on the outside and a little pink in the middle. Cook in batches, transferring the cooked liver to a warm platter loosely covered with aluminum foil.
- **Sauce, "The Method":** Reduce the heat under the frying pan and allow it to cool a minute before adding capers, 1 tablespoon chopped shallots, and vinegar. Boil and reduce the vinegar until syrupy; then add the beef stock and reduce by half. Remove the pan from the heat and add the cold butter piece by piece, while whisking vigorously and shaking the pan. Stir in the chopped parsley.
- Arrange the liver on serving plates and spoon some sauce over each portion. Yield: 4 servings.

Chew on This

This film was originally called *Hot Lunch*.

Food for Thought

Many of the teachers featured in this film were actual drama, music, and dance teachers at the time the film was shot.

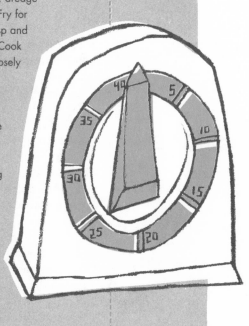

Steaming Pork Buns with "Oh, what a filling"

We guarantee that once you bite through this steamy bun and into the succulent pork within, you'll want to cut the necks out of all your T-shirts, slip on a pair of leg warmers, and douse yourself with a bucket of cold water.

For the Buns
¾ cup lukewarm water
1 Tbsp active dry yeast
2 Tbsp sugar
1 Tbsp vegetable oil
1 Tbsp sesame oil
2½ cups flour
1 sweat shirt, strategically ripped

For the Pork
8 oz pork tenderloin, cut in ¼-inch cubes
2 Tbsp soy sauce, mixed with 1 Tbsp corn starch
1 Tbsp dry sherry
2 scallions, minced
1 tsp ginger, grated
1 tsp garlic, minced
2 Tbsp hoisin sauce
1 Tbsp sugar
1 Tbsp peanut oil

Food for Thought

Don't have a steamer? Improvise with a colander or flat strainer balanced on ramekins (small oven-proof bowls).

- **Get those buns moving:** In a small bowl, combine the warm water, yeast, sugar, and the oils. Whisk vigorously and set aside in a warm place until the yeast begins to bubble, about 10 minutes.
- Sift 2 cups of flour into a medium mixing bowl. Gradually pour in the water and

yeast mixture, stirring with a wooden spoon until the dough forms a cohesive mass.

- Turn the dough out onto a lightly floured surface and knead for 5 minutes, adding only as much flour as needed to keep the dough from sticking.
- Place the dough in an oiled bowl, cover with plastic wrap and set aside in a warm spot until double in bulk, about 45 minutes.
- While the dough rises, combine the pork with the soy, sherry, scallion, ginger, garlic, hoisin sauce, and sugar.
- Heat peanut in a wok or heavy skillet over high heat. Add the pork mixture and stir fry 2–3 minutes. Remove from heat and cool to room temperature.

- Remove dough to a lightly floured board and roll into a cylinder, 2 inches wide and 12 inches long. Cut into 12 pieces; flatten each piece into a 3-inch disc.
- Place 2 Tbsp of filling in the center of each disc. Gather the dough around the filling in small pleats; twist and pinch together to seal.
- Place each of the buns on a small sheet of foil or parchment, cover with a damp cloth and let rise 30 minutes in a warm spot.
- Arrange in a single layer on a plate or steamer basket and steam 10–15 minutes over rapidly boiling water. Eat warm or let cool to room temperature, wrap, and refrigerate.
- **End up with pork buns of steel?** Don't fret if your buns don't puff as proudly as you'd like, they'll still be hot and tasty (and you can always call in your pork bun stand-in for the close-ups). Yield: 12 steaming buns.

INSIDE SCOOP

When this movie first came out, Jennifer Beals stunned the moviegoing public by demonstrating the complicated process involved in removing one's bra without removing one's sweatshirt.

Whoopie's B-Flat Flatbread

This recipe for easy party snacks was born in a cross-fire hurricane, but we recommend using a kitchen.

For the Flatbread
1½ cups water
½ tsp salt
1 onion, roughly chopped
1½ cups bulgur wheat
1½–2 cups all-purpose flour, divided

For the Garbanzo Dip
1 15-oz can garbanzo beans
4 Tbsp sesame seeds, crushed
1 Tbsp sesame oil
¼ cup freshly squeezed lemon juice
2 cloves garlic, mashed with salt
Olive oil, cumin, and cayenne
  to garnish

For the Chili-Mint Salsa
1 cucumber, peeled, seeded, and diced
2 ripe tomatoes, diced
½ cup chopped flat-leaf parsley
3 serrano or jalapeño peppers, minced
¼ cup chopped mint leaves
3 Tbsp rice-wine vinegar
Salt and pepper

For the Eggplant-Yogurt Spread
1 large firm eggplant
1 whole head garlic, unpeeled
1 cup plain yogurt
3 Tbsp extra virgin olive oil
1 Tbsp freshly squeezed lemon juice
Salt and pepper
1 pair Jagger wax lips (tongue
  optional)

INSIDE SCOOP

Archeologists tell us that unleavened flat-bread and crushed garbanzos were the earliest foods prepared by ancient man, 5,000 years before the birth of Christ.

"I've been around ten years–a very long flash-in-the-pan. More like a kitchen fire."

—Whoopi Goldberg shortly before hosting the 1993 Academy Awards

• **Make the dough:** Combine the water, salt, and onion in the jar of a blender and blend until smooth. Pour the mixture into a small saucepan and bring to a boil. Place the bulgur in a medium mixing bowl, pour the hot liquid over the bulgur and set aside for 15 minutes.

- Add 1 cup flour to the bulgur and stir with a wooden spoon until incorporated. Transfer the dough onto a floured board, put "Jumpin' Jack Flash" on the stereo, and begin kneading. Add more flour only as needed to keep the dough from sticking. When the song is over, stop kneading only long enough to play it again from the top. The second time the song is finished so is the dough. Stop kneading. Cover the dough with a damp cloth and let rest for 30 minutes.
- **Make the dip:** Combine garbanzo beans, sesame seeds, sesame oil, lemon juice, and garlic in the work bowl of a food processor and process until smooth and well blended. Spread onto a dish, drizzle olive oil in a trough down the center, and dust with cayenne and cumin.
- **Make the salsa:** Combine cucumber, tomatoes, parsley, peppers, mint, and vinegar in a serving bowl. Season to taste with salt and pepper.
- **Make the spread:** Preheat oven to 425°F. Pierce the eggplant with a skewer in half a dozen places; wrap the garlic in foil. Place both on a baking sheet and roast for 30–45 minutes (leave oven on). Peel the eggplant under cold water. Transfer to a colander and press out any bitter juices. Cut the garlic in half and squeeze into a mixing bowl (discard peeling). Place the eggplant in the bowl with the roasted garlic and mash with a fork until smooth. Fold in the the yogurt, olive oil, and lemon. Season to taste with salt and pepper.
- **Bake the flatbread:** Evenly divide the dough into 12 pieces. Roll each piece out as thinly as possible. Lay out flat on a lightly floured baking sheet and bake on the floor or lowest shelf of the hot oven for 2 minutes. Flip and bake for 1 additional minute.
- Eat the hot B-flat flatbreads right out of the oven by tearing off a piece and scooping it into one or more of the sauces. Yield: 6 servings.

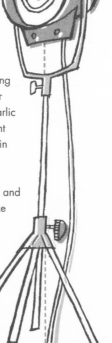

Food for Thought

If you wanna b sharp, don't b flat; just b natural.

● **A Tip From Mick Jagger:** "Always pace yourself and don't eat too fast, 'cuz eating on the run gives you gas, gas, gas."

Blues Brothers Funky Chicken

It's ten feet to the kitchen, we have a fryer full of oil, a bag of chicken, it's night, and we're wearing chef's hats.

For the Buttermilk Marinade
8 garlic cloves, finely chopped
1 tsp fresh thyme, chopped
1 tsp fresh oregano, chopped
1 Tbsp Tabasco sauce
3 cups buttermilk
1 cup ice

For the Coating
3 cups all-purpose flour
½ cup cornmeal
2 tsp black pepper
2 tsp salt
1 Tbsp paprika

Food for Thought

When breading the chicken pieces, use only one hand in case you get a phone call.

For the Funky Chicken
Canola oil, as needed
1 large scoop soul (or soul substitute)
8 boneless chicken thighs (feel free to substitute white meat if desired, you can always pretend it's dark)

- Mix together the garlic, thyme, oregano, Tabasco, buttermilk, and ice.
- Cover the chicken with the buttermilk mixture and refrigerate.
- In a large, shallow dish, combine the flour, cornmeal, black pepper, salt, and paprika.
- Fill a large, heavy skillet with canola oil to a depth of ½–1 inch. If using an electric fry pan, set the temperature anywhere from 360°F to 370°F.

- If cooking on the stove top, place the pan over medium-high heat. (Check the temperature by dropping a cube of bread into the oil; it should take about a minute to brown.)
- Remove chicken from the buttermilk and dredge each piece in the flour mixture; shake off the excess. Dip again into the buttermilk, then one last time into the flour. If working with limited counter space, the flour mixture can be shaken on in a paper bag.
- Lay that funky chicken down into the hot oil without crowding or touching. Frying too many pieces at once will cause the oil to cool down and the chicken will end up greasy. Fry each piece for a total of 20–25 minutes, turning often.
- If frying more than one batch of chicken, keep cooked pieces warm on a baking sheet in a 250°F oven. Yield: 4 servings.

Funky Tip:

You can be the Godfather of Soul Food! After wowing your guests with one funky dish after another, drape your sweat-soaked apron over your shoulders like a cape and have someone lead you dramatically out of the kitchen. (For added effect, mop your forehead while declaring, "I can't cook no mo'.") Do this between each course until it's time to do the dishes, then disappear completely. **Whoa!**

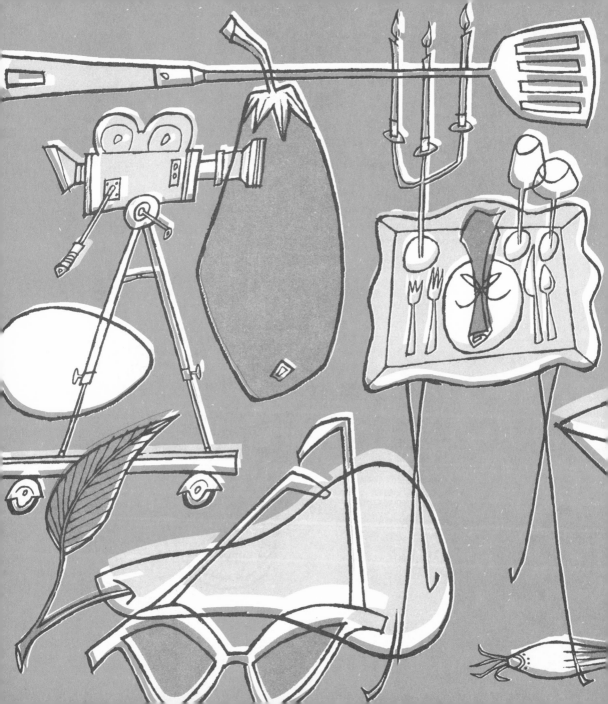

Road Trip

Breaker, Breaker
Banana Cream Pie

After doubling down on a double nickel across five state lines, nothing says 10-4 like a slice of truck-stop–style banana cream pie.

For the Pie Crust
1½ cups chocolate wafers, finely ground
¼ cup butter, melted
1 tsp ground cinnamon
1 Tbsp egg white, beaten

For the Filling
¾ cup sugar
5 Tbsp cornstarch
¼ tsp salt
3 cups half-and-half
4 egg yolks, beaten
4 Tbsp butter
1½ tsp vanilla
5 firm, ripe bananas
Juice of 1 lemon

For the Topping
2 cups whipping cream
½ cup flaked coconut, toasted
1 clever and irreverent CB handle to help elevate you to folk-hero status
1 persistent Smokey on your tail

- **Make the crust:** Preheat oven to 350°F. In a large bowl, combine the ground wafers, melted butter, cinnamon, and beaten egg white. Stir with a fork until

Did You Know?

Burt Reynolds was the top-grossing box office star from 1978–1982

Chew on This

Trans Am, what's your pleasure? This car had its debut in 1969, and the year after *Smokey and the Bandit* was released, its popularity soared. By 1979, manufacturing was up 75 percent.

evenly mixed and well moistened.

- Empty the crust mixture into a buttered 9-inch pie plate. Spread and pat mixture evenly over the sides and bottom of the pie plate and bake 8–10 minutes until firm.
- **Make the filling:** In a medium, heavy-bottomed saucepan, sift together the sugar, cornstarch, and salt. Slowly whisk in the half-and-half and the egg yolks; continue whisking until creamy and free of lumps.
- Place the egg mixture over medium heat and slowly bring to a boil while whisking constantly. Reduce heat to a low simmer and continue to whisk and cook another 2–3 minutes until thickened. Never Stop Whisking.
- Pour the hot mixture into a mixing bowl and stir in the vanilla and butter. Cover with plastic wrap and set aside to cool for 20 minutes. The plastic wrap should be placed directly on the pudding surface to prevent a skin from forming.
- Peel the bananas, slice into ¼-inch rounds, and toss with the lemon juice.
- **Fill the pie:** Spread a third of the filling in the bottom of the pie crust and arrange half of the sliced bananas evenly over the filling. Spread another third of the filling over the banana layer and top with the remaining bananas. Top with the remaining filling and dust with a little of the toasted coconut. Refrigerate at least 1½ hours, or until the filling has set.
- **Top it off:** Combine the cream and the remaining coconut and whip until thickened but not stiff. Spoon coconut cream over each slice and eat rapidly. Yield: one 9-inch pie.
- Finish your coffee, tip the waitress, and hop back in your 18-wheeler. And remember, good buddy, old truckers never die, they just get a new Peterbilt.

Thai Noodles with Airplane Nuts

When we think flying, we think nuts. This high-flying recipe uses plenty of 'em, and with the cost of airline tickets, these crunchy, in-flight treats don't come cheap. So next time you fly, hold onto your nuts. And don't call us Shirley.

For the Noodles
2 chicken breasts, skinless and boneless

2 Tbsp dry sherry

3 Tbsp soy sauce

¼ cup peanut oil

5 cloves garlic, finely chopped

1 serrano or jalapeño pepper, finely chopped

1 Tbsp shredded pickled ginger

2 eggs, beaten

1 cup (or 8 flight-sized bags) peanuts, coarsely chopped

½ yellow bell pepper, sliced into ½-inch strips

1 cup mung bean sprouts

½ lb spaghetti or vermicelli

1 Tbsp sugar

2 Tbsp fish sauce (if unavailable, use anchovy paste)

1 Tbsp catsup

3 scallions, cut into 1-inch lengths

For the Garnish
3 limes, cut into quarters

1 tsp red pepper flakes

¼ cup peanuts, crushed

¼ cup mint leaves, roughly chopped

¼ cup cilantro leaves

1 air-sickness bag (for leftovers)

Chew on This

"*Spartacus* is considered the greatest gladiator movie of all time."

—Captain Oveur
honorary chairman,
Cloak and Sandal Society

- Slice the chicken into thin strips and place in a small bowl. Add the sherry and half of the soy sauce. Cover, set aside, and remember, everyone is counting on you.
- Cook the pasta *al dente*. Rinse well in cold water, drain, and set aside.
- Prepare and lay out all ingredients where they can be reached quickly during the stir fry. Avoid touching eyes and sensitive areas of self and others after cutting chile peppers.
- Using a wok or large cast-iron skillet, heat the peanut oil on high heat. Add the garlic, serrano pepper, and pickled ginger and stir fry until light brown and fragrant.
- Drain excess marinade from chicken and add to the wok along with the beaten eggs. Stir fry for 2 minutes and remember, everyone is counting on you.
- Run cold water on any blistered areas of face or hands from oil splatters in steps 4 and 5.
- Add the bell pepper, pasta, and half of the bean sprouts. Stir fry for another minute, and remember, everyone is counting on you.
- Add the remaining soy sauce, peanuts, catsup, fish sauce, and sugar. Cook for another minute, stirring often.
- Mix in the scallions and transfer to a serving platter. Garnish with the remaining bean sprouts, fresh mint, cilantro, lime quarters, red pepper flakes, and peanuts.
- At this point your guests may begin to smell something wonderful coming from the kitchen, and wonder what it is. (A large room with pots, pans, and a stove, but that's not important right now.) Yield: 4 servings.

INSIDE SCOOP

Peanut oil is the oil most often used by Chinese chefs for wok cooking because it can be heated to well over 400°F before it smokes or burns.

Seafood 'n' Eat It Stew

Ahh, the sound of the surf, the far-off cries of a sea gull, the feel of warm sand between your toes. Pack your bags, it's going to be great. . . .

For the Stew

2 cups water

2 cups dry white wine or vermouth

2 12-oz bottles clam juice

2 whole bay leaves

5 whole black peppercorns

2 onions, diced

2 carrots, diced

2 stalks celery, diced

10 whole cloves of garlic, peeled and chopped

3 Tbsp olive oil

3 cups tomatoes, chopped (or 1 28-oz can)

Juice and zest of one lemon

½ tsp cayenne pepper

2 tsp dried basil

Salt and pepper

2½–3 lbs of assorted shellfish and white-fleshed fish (such as shrimp, lobster, red snapper, halibut, scallops, sea bass, clams, mussels, etc.)

Italian parsley, finely chopped

2 weeks worth of vacation

1 week's worth of traveler's checks

1 car full of screaming kids

WARNING:

This recipe contains no VHF and UHF ray block whatsoever. Please use at your own risk.

- **See the seafood:** Shell shrimp and reserve shells, scrub clams and mussels, cut lobster and fish into large chunks.
- **Make the broth:** In a large, heavy saucepan or pot, combine the water, wine, clam juice, bay leaves, and peppercorns with half of the following: onions,

Did You Know?

• John Candy won Emmy® awards in 1982 and 1983 for his writing of SCTV's comedy sketches.

• Rip Torn has appeared in more than 80 films. His debut was in the 1956 Tennessee Williams classic *Baby Doll*.

carrots, celery, and garlic, plus all the reserved shrimp shells. Bring to a boil, reduce heat, and simmer at least 30 minutes. Strain, discard solids, and reserve the stock.

- **Make the stew:** Using the same pot, heat the olive oil and add the remaining onions, carrots, celery, and garlic. Cook over medium heat for 5 minutes; add the tomatoes, lemon juice and zest, cayenne, and basil; simmer 20 minutes. Add the reserved stock to the tomato base and return to a boil. Add salt and freshly cracked black pepper to taste. If using lobster, mussels, clams, or crab, add these first and simmer 3 minutes. Remove the clams and mussels as they open. Add the remaining fish, scallops, or shrimp and simmer 5 more minutes, until just cooked through.
- **Eat it:** Ladle into bowls, top with clams and mussels, and garnish with chopped parsley. Serve with hot slices of garlic toast.

  Yield: 6 servings.
- Eat, drink, and be merry, and don't dwell on the fact that when your vacation's over, you'll be broke, exhausted, and really need a vacation.

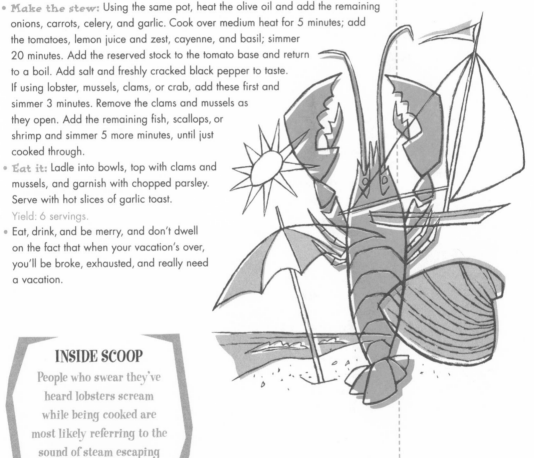

INSIDE SCOOP

People who swear they've heard lobsters scream while being cooked are most likely referring to the sound of steam escaping from the shell.

Award-Winning Clams Casino

In the 1950s clams on the half shell were a standard complimentary item in many casinos. That way, you could eat with one hand and lose money with the other. Our recipe for Clams Casino is a sure bet. Even Raymond would like 'em—about a hundred of 'em.

½ lb bacon
¼ cup onions, minced
3 cloves garlic, minced
1 small yellow bell pepper, finely diced
1 small red bell pepper, finely diced
1 jalapeño pepper, very finely diced
8 oz butter, softened
¼ cup parsley, finely chopped
2 Tbsp lemon juice
2 Tbsp vermouth
1 pinch cayenne pepper
Salt and pepper to taste
24 Cherrystone, Topneck, or Pismo clams
1 copy television schedule (You never know when Wapner might move to a different time slot.)

- Scrub clams with a vegetable brush and soak in salted water (⅓ cup salt to 1 gallon of water) for one hour.
- Dice half of the bacon and cook until crispy. Drain all but 1 tablespoon of the fat from the skillet, then add the onions, garlic, bell pepper, and jalapeño; sauté until tender. Remove from heat and set aside to cool.
- In a medium mixing bowl, mix the butter until smooth and creamy. Add the cooled bacon mixture, parsley, lemon juice, vermouth, cayenne, salt, and pepper. Mix until all ingredients are evenly combined.
- Lay out a 16-inch sheet of foil on a flat working surface. Transfer the butter

Food for Thought

If you don't have a clam knife, don't panic. Try using a church-key-style can opener, running over the clams with your car, or hiring an otter.

CLAM FACTS

When buying clams, make sure their shells are tightly closed. Never store clams in a sealed plastic bag— they'll suffocate.

mixture onto the foil and roll tightly into a cylinder. Refrigerate.

- Arrange the remaining bacon on a cutting board. Using a cookie cutter or paring knife, cut out 24 little poker chips and award statuettes. Bring enough water to a boil in a small saucepan to blanch the bacon cutouts for 5 minutes. Drain and set aside.
- **Preheat broiler.** Open the clams and loosen the meat from the shells. Lay clams out on a shallow baking pan. Top each with a slice of the chilled butter mixture and a piece of blanched bacon.
- Broil until the bacon just begins to get crisp. Don't overcook or the clams will get tough. Yield: 24 big ones.

Easy Pop Quiz:

Divide the total number of clams by the number of letters in "Wapner," and multiply by the number of ounces of butter used in this recipe. What is the square root of the remainder? (Answer below.)

Answer: 5.6566784

INSIDE SCOOP

· *Rain Man* won a total of 4 Academy Awards.

· All throughout the movie Raymond (played by Dustin Hoffman) is taking photographs. They are featured at the end of the movie underneath the credits.

Campfire Grilled Vegetable Salad

Nothing beats the wilderness for getting away from it all. You leave the workaday week behind to rough it, commune with nature, and enjoy all the sounds of the forest: the wind in the trees, the hoot of an owl, the babbling brook, the theme song from Dinner & a Movie blasting from the surround-sound of the big-screen TV you packed in with you to the campsite. Sure, getting back to nature is great, but you can't miss the show.

Chew on This

Want a grilled vegetable soup instead of salad? After the vegetables have been grilled and cut into pieces, cover with a rich chicken or vegetable stock and simmer for 20-30 minutes. Season to taste with salt and pepper and garnish with chopped parsley.

2 red bell peppers
2 yellow bell peppers
2 Japanese eggplants
2 small yellow squash
2 small zucchini
1 red onion
2 bunches leeks
1 cup extra virgin olive oil
¼ cup chopped flat-leaf parsley
8–10 cloves garlic, minced
¼ cup cider vinegar
2 tsp cumin seed, toasted and ground
Salt and pepper
1 bottle calamine lotion
1 copy sheet music to "Kumbaya"
1 very long extension cord for television

INSIDE SCOOP

Louis Jourdan sings the "Dinner & a Movie" theme, "Beans and Cornbread."

- **Prepare the salad fixins:** Cut the peppers in half lengthwise, trim off the white membrane and remove the seeds. Slice the Japanese eggplant, yellow squash, and zucchini lengthwise into ½-inch slices. Peel the red onion and slice into ½-inch rounds. Trim the root bundle and the dark green ends from the leeks, slice in half lengthwise, and rinse well in an icy mountain stream (or under the tap). Wrap the leeks in foil and set aside.

- In a small bowl, whisk together the olive oil, parsley, and garlic. Brush the sliced vegetables lightly with the mixture.
- Prepare a good-sized charcoal or mesquite fire. Allow it to burn down to ash-topped coals before arranging the coals evenly throughout the fire pit. For about a minute look around for a wire brush to clean the grill; then give up and use a paper towel like always.
- Working in batches, grill the vegetables on both sides until nicely marked. Depending on the intensity of the fire, figure about 2–3 minutes per side, with the exception of the leeks, which should cook for 5 minutes in their foil jackets before being unwrapped and grilled.
- Cut the grilled vegetables into 2- to 3-inch pieces and place in a large mixing bowl. Add the vinegar and cumin to the olive oil mixture and whisk together. Pour the dressing over the warm vegetables and toss. Transfer to a platter, season with salt and pepper, and serve.

Yield: 4–6 servings.

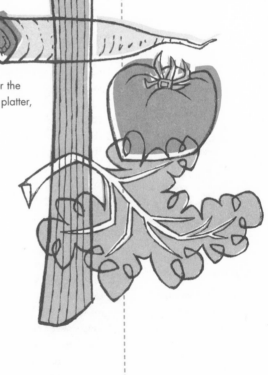

Experts Agree:
For the best flavor when cooking outdoors, always use as much "borrowed" wood as possible from neighboring cabins and campsites.

Bluto's Beer Chili

You're invited to join the Delta house for one rousing, out-of-control chili recipe made with plenty of ice-cold beer. Don't worry, though, most of the alcohol burns off during cooking, so you won't land on double-secret probation.

3 Tbsp corn oil
2 lbs skirt steak, cut into ½-inch cubes
2 lbs pork sausage
10 cloves garlic, minced
2 medium onions, roughly chopped
2 jalapeño peppers, seeded and finely diced
2 Tbsp ground cumin
1 Tbsp ground coriander
5 Tbsp chili powder
1 Tbsp paprika
1 tsp chili flakes
2 tsp oregano
1 tsp sage
1 bell pepper, diced
2 stalks celery, diced
1 28-oz can crushed tomatoes
1 6-oz can roasted chilis, blended or finely chopped
2 cups beef stock
1 bay leaf
2 tsp salt
4 cups pinto or black beans, fully cooked (optional)
2 Tbsp fine cornmeal or *masa harina* (optional)
8 25-gal kegs of beer, ice cold . . . okay, 2 12-oz cans of beer
   (can't blame a guy for trying)

Extra Credit

Worried about passing Home Ec? You can make yourself a toga by using three rolls of paper towel and some duct tape. You just might get an A. In any case, you'll be dressed for the movie and very absorbent.

Chew on This

BEAN TIP

#237

The process of soaking dried beans overnight before cooking helps eliminate the compounds that cause audible, gastrointestinal turbulence. During Delta pledge week, please disregard.

- In a large cast-iron skillet, heat the oil on medium-high heat until quite hot and lightly brown the meat. Brown in three or four batches to avoid overcrowding the skillet.
- Transfer the browned meat to a large dutch oven or heavy casserole. Discard all but 3 Tbsp of fat from the skillet.
- Reduce the heat under the skillet to medium and add the garlic, onions, and diced jalapeño peppers. Sauté for 2 minutes, stirring often.
- Add the cumin, coriander, chili powder, paprika, chili flakes, oregano, and sage to the skillet; stir well to coat the onions, garlic, and jalapeños with the spices.
- Continue cooking the spice mixture for another minute, stirring frequently to avoid scorching.
- Add the bell pepper, celery, crushed tomatoes with their juice, and the canned chilis. Stir well with a wooden spoon, scraping the bottom and sides to loosen any tasty bits stuck to the skillet. Transfer contents of the skillet to the dutch oven and place over medium-high heat.
- Add the beef stock, bay leaf, salt, and beer to the dutch oven, stirring well to mix all the ingredients.
- Bring the chili to a boil. Reduce the heat to low, and with the pot half covered cook at a simmer 1–2 hours, until the meat is tender.
- If you are adding beans: When the meat is tender, add the cooked beans and simmer another 20 minutes. Hot beans may also be held on the side and added by request.
- *Note:* If you want the chili to be a little thicker, add the cornmeal or *masa harina* a little at a time, stirring constantly. This will thicken up the chili and add a subtle, earthy flavor. Yield: 12–16 servings (enough for the whole frat).

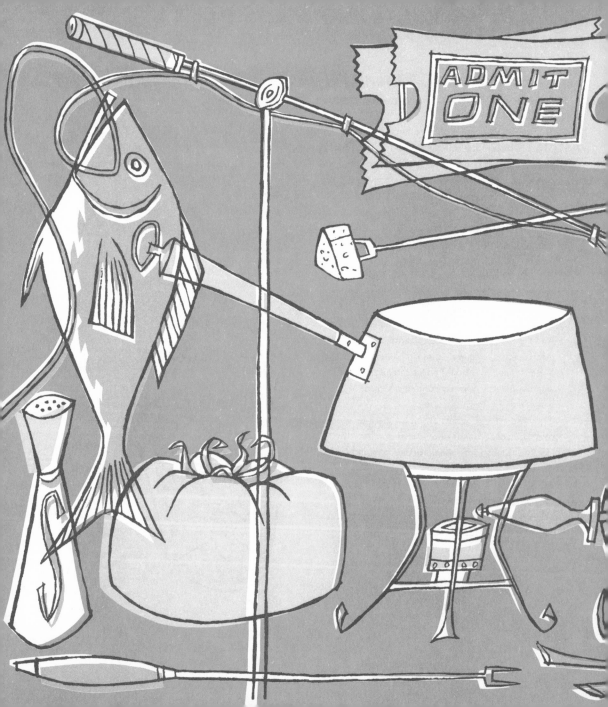

Cold
War

Nuclear-Sub Sandwiches with Russian Dressing

Be a hero in your own kitchen! Like our young David Lightman and the W.O.P.R., try programming your microwave to understand the futility of culinary thermonuclear confrontation (always embarrassing when guests are over). Modern household appliances should always be used for good, never evil.

Russian Dressing
4 Tbsp sun-dried tomatoes,
   pureed or finely minced
½ cup mayonnaise
2 tsp lemon juice
1 green onion, minced

Olive Tapenade
1 cup oil-cured black olives, pitted
¼ tsp crushed red pepper
1–2 cloves garlic, minced
2 Tbsp capers
1 fresh thyme sprig, finely chopped
⅛ cup extra virgin olive oil

The Sub
2 half chicken breasts,
   skinned and boned
1 Tbsp olive oil
2 sprigs fresh rosemary
½ cup water
2 yellow bell peppers
¼ lb prosciutto, thinly sliced
¼ lb provolone, thinly sliced
2 large, ripe tomatoes, thinly sliced
1 (war)head butter lettuce
2 loaves baguette-style French bread
1 bowl microchips, well salted

Chew on This

Russian dressing was invented in 1940 at Delmonico's restaurant in New York City.

- **Prepare the dressing of the former Soviet Union:** Combine all dressing ingredients, mix well, cover, and refrigerate.
- **Prepare the tapenade:** If using a food processor, combine all tapenade ingredients, and process the mixture briefly (just 2 or 3 pulses). If chopping by hand, combine olives, garlic, and capers on a board and chop together roughly. Transfer to a bowl, add thyme and olive oil, and mix with a wooden spoon.

Food for Thought

Why didn't they just unplug the computer?

- **Cook the chicken breasts:** Season chicken breasts with a little salt and pepper. Add the olive oil to a small sauté pan and heat over medium-high heat. Place the chicken in the pan smooth-side down and sauté for 2–3 minutes, until nicely browned. Reduce heat to medium-low and turn the breasts over. Place a rosemary sprig on each breast, add the water, and cover. Continue cooking for another 10 minutes, or until the meat is firm to the touch. Remove pan from heat and let the chicken cool in the broth. When cool enough to handle, slice chicken on the diagonal as thinly as possible and set aside.
- **Roast the peppers:** Preheat broiler. Rub whole peppers lightly with a tiny bit of olive oil and place under the broiler as close to the heat as possible. Using long tongs, turn every minute until the skin on all sides is black and blistered. Transfer the roasted peppers to a paper bag, close the top, and let cool for 5 minutes. Remove peppers from the bag and, while holding them under running water, rub the burnt skin off and remove the seeds and white membrane. Dry the peppers, cut lengthwise into 1-inch strips, and set aside.
- **Construct the sandwich:** Cut the baguettes in half lengthwise. Spread the olive tapenade over the cut side of the bottom half and the dressing of the former Soviet Union over the cut side of the top. Building from bottom to top, construct your sub with chicken, peppers, prosciutto, provolone, tomatoes, and lettuce. Complete the subs with the top piece of bread and cut each baguette into 4–6 pieces. Yield: 4-6 servings.

> Just think, had we launched this sub at the Soviets in the spirit of gastronomic glasnost, neither of our countries would be flat broke now.
> ## Make snacks, not war!

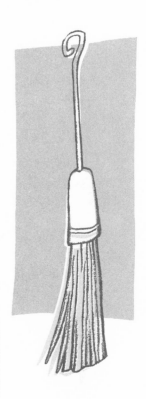

OO7 Martini Fondue

In the seventies, a bubbling fondue pot was synonymous with penthouse parties and worldly sophistication. Although the word is derived from the original French "to melt," we prefer the direct translation: "If you heat the cheese, they will come."

1½ pounds Swiss cheese
3 Tbsp flour
1 clove garlic
1 Tbsp butter
1 cup champagne
½ tsp white pepper
1 pinch cayenne pepper
1 pinch nutmeg
½ tsp lemon zest
½ cup green olives, thinly sliced
1 ounce vodka
1 loaf or baguette of French bread
1 savagely depraved, but impossibly brilliant, superfoe
1 top-secret spy watch that converts to a handy whisk watch
No real plan to speak of .

- Grate or chop the cheese as finely as possible. Toss with the flour and set aside.
- Rub inside of the fondue pot or earthenware casserole first with the clove of garlic, then with the butter.
- Place the pot over a medium-high heat and add the champagne. Heat until just boiling. Add the floured cheese a handful at a time, stirring with a wooden spoon after each addition.
- When the cheese is melted and creamy, add the white and cayenne peppers, nutmeg, lemon zest, and olives. Bring the mixture to a boil, stir in the vodka, and reduce the heat to a simmer (or transfer to a fondue warmer).

THINGS
YOU NEVER
HEAR
JAMES BOND
SAY:

- Stirred not shaken.

- Can I get this in a doggie bag?

- This thing's goin' too fast for me!

- Cut the French bread into small cubes, each with a bit of crust attached. Serve in a basket.
- Save the human race: Being the crack spy you are, suddenly you realize that you've been double-crossed. These are not bread cubes at all, but little nuclear devices! You have only moments to skewer them swiftly and deftly, dip them in your anti-bomb cheese sauce, and eat rapidly. (Followed by a martini, of course. You might be stirred, but you're never shaken. Oh, James!)

Yield: 4–6 servings.

INSIDE SCOOP
Fondue was originally created by European goatherds to use up stale bread and old cheese.

Real Men's Quiche

Who cares if real men don't eat quiche? It takes a real man to make one entirely from scratch, especially when being chased by Soviet agents.

For the Shell
1½ cups all-purpose flour
½ tsp salt
1 tsp sugar
4 oz butter, chilled and cut into pieces
2 Tbsp vegetable shortening, chilled
1 large egg, chilled
3 Tbsp ice water

For the Filling
4 eggs
1½ cups half-and-half
1 tsp red pepper flakes
½ tsp black pepper
½ tsp oregano
½ tsp salt
¼ cup fresh basil, chopped
1 cup hot Italian sausage, cooked and crumbled
1 7-oz can roasted chilis, thinly sliced
½ cup Jack cheese, shredded
1 cup Cheddar cheese, shredded
1 ripe tomato, thinly sliced
1 fully loaded index finger (silencer optional)

- **Be a man and make the shell yourself:** In the bowl of a food processor, combine the flour, salt, sugar, and butter. Pulse 4 times to roughly combine the ingredients. Add the butter, shortening, and the egg and pulse the machine 5–6

INSIDE SCOOP

When making any type of pie shell, handle the dough as little as possible. Overkneading increases the gluten structure and can make the pastry tough.

more times until the dough resembles small peas. Add the ice water and pulse another couple of times. Scrape dough onto a clean work surface and knead once or twice by hand. Shape into a 5-inch disc; wrap in plastic and refrigerate at least 20 minutes.

- **Roll it out and bake it (if you can take it):** Preheat the oven to 425°F. Roll out the dough evenly to a diameter of approximately 13 inches. Turn an 8-inch cake pan upside down and butter all surfaces. Transfer the dough to the outside surface of the pan and trim any overhanging edges. Flute the edges with the tines of a fork. Keeping the pan upside down, slide it into the oven and bake for 10 minutes.
- Remove from oven and cool at least 15 minutes before inverting and removing the cake pan from the shell.
- **Get a little rough:** In a mixing bowl, combine the eggs, half-and-half, pepper flakes, black pepper, oregano, salt, and basil and beat well.
- **Fill it up:** Place the shell on a cookie sheet. Sprinkle the sausage and one-half of each cheese into the pastry shell. Fill with the egg mixture to ¼-inch of the rim and arrange the roasted chilis on top. Reduce the oven temperature to 375°F.
- **Can you take the heat?** Sprinkle quiche with remaining cheese and arrange the tomato slices over the top. Bake for about 40 minutes, until puffy and nicely browned. Yield: 6–8 servings.
- Cut into slices and stand proudly with arms akimbo while your adoring guests enjoy the meal.

Chew on This

Real Men star John Ritter is the son of singing country stars Tex Ritter and Dorothy Fay.

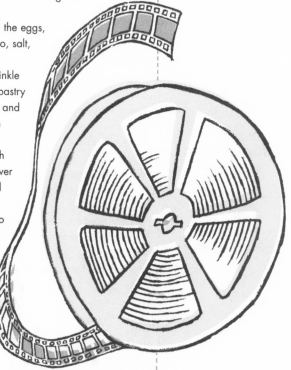

Iced Cold War Martinis and Secret Spy Snacks

This 1985 Bond film gives Roger Moore barely enough time to eat. These Cold War snacks can be assembled quickly, eaten on the run, and chased down with the quintessential Bond dry martini.

For the Iced Cold War Martinis
Cracked ice
12 oz vodka
1½ oz dry vermouth
1 lemon

For the Lemon Cream
½ cup whipping cream
½ cup sour cream
2 tsp lemon juice

For the Parmesan Twists
1 sheet frozen puff pastry
1 egg, beaten with 1 Tbsp milk
½ cup grated Parmesan cheese
1 tsp sesame seeds

For the Secret Spy Snacks
4 small red potatoes, cooked
  and chilled
1 English cucumber
12 cherry tomatoes
2 oz smoked salmon
2 oz smoked chicken
2 oz Beluga caviar
1 bunch fresh dill
1 tuxedo
1 license to kill (or learner's permit,
  if accompanied by a licensed
  killer over 18)

- **Have an Iced Cold War Martini:** Fill a mixing glass with cracked ice. Measure in the vodka and vermouth. **Shake**, do not stir. Strain into iced glasses.
- **Make the lemon twists:** Cut two thin strips of lemon peel. Release their essential oils by firmly grasping the ends and rotating either hand anywhere from 110° to 180°, depending on the amount of extraction desired. Rub lemon twists around the rims of the glasses before depositing dead center in each glass and offering a toast to Her Majesty, the Queen.

- **Make the lemon cream:** Whip the cream until soft peaks form. Fold in the sour cream and lemon juice; cover and refrigerate 20 minutes.
- **Make the Parmesan twists:** Preheat oven to 400°F. Lay out puff pastry and brush with the egg mixture. Sprinkle with the Parmesan and sesame seeds. Cut the sheet into ½-inch-wide strips and twist a few times. Bake for 10–15 minutes, until golden.
- **Prepare the Secret Spy Snacks:** Slice the potatoes and cucumber into ½-inch rounds. Using a melon baller or small spoon, scoop out a shallow indentation in the center of each slice (being careful not to go all the way through the slice).
- Remove the stems from the cherry tomatoes. Balance each tomato upside down on its shoulders and cut a slice off of round bottom (which is now, of course, the top). Scoop out the seeds and pulp with a small spoon.
- Fill the prepared potato, cucumber, and tomato bases with smoked fish, smoked chicken, or caviar. Top with cold lemon cream and garnish with a small sprig of dill.
- Serve with the Parmesan twists and a second round of martinis. Yield: 4 servings.

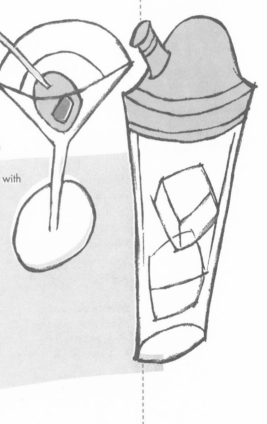

INSIDE SCOOP
This is Roger Moore's last appearance as 007.

Secret Agent Party Tip:
Hide politically explosive microfilm in one of the spy snacks. Whoever finds it must effortlessly pummel the largest guest, seduce the hostess, and leave without using the door.

Be All That
You Can Beef Stroganoff

Listen up, troops! The mission on which you are about to embark is not child's play. Some of you will get burned. Some of you will spill stuff on your pants. And some of you, God forbid, may even mis-measure the amount of nutmeg in the sauce. But at the end of the day, you'll be able to look at yourself in the mirror and say, "I'm a lean, mean cooking machine." Dismissed!

Chew on This

MUSHROOM TIP
#6

Mushrooms are tricky. When being sautéed, they initially absorb the oil in the pan. Keep cooking and watch for the oil to reappear. When it does, they're done.

For the Beef
2 lbs beef tenderloin, trimmed and cut into 1-inch slices
1 bay leaf, crushed
½ onion, thinly sliced
¼ cup dry vermouth
Salt and pepper

For the Mushrooms and Onions
3 Tbsp butter
3 Tbsp olive oil
½ lb mushrooms, quartered
¾ cup pearl onions, peeled

Did You Know?

Bill Murray and Harold Ramis were part of Chicago's Second City improvisational troupe. Both starred in another successful feature, *Ghostbusters.*

For the Sauce
2 Tbsp shallots, finely chopped
½ cup beef broth
⅓ cup dry vermouth
⅛ tsp nutmeg
¼ cup heavy cream
1 cup sour cream
2 Tbsp chopped parsley
1 shingle (optional)

- **Marinate the meat, SIR:** In a large mixing bowl, combine the bay leaf, onion, and vermouth. Add beef, stir to coat, cover, and set aside for 20 minutes.
- **Sauté the mushrooms and onions, SIR:** In a large, heavy skillet over medium-high heat, add 1 tablespoon each of the butter and olive oil. Add the mushrooms and sauté until light brown, about 3 minutes. Add the pearl onions to the pan with the mushrooms and continue sautéing 2 more minutes. Transfer the mushrooms and onions to a warm dish. Wipe the pan out, add the remaining butter and olive oil, and return to the heat.
- **Sauté the beef, SIR:** Remove the meat from the marinade and dry well with a paper towel. Season lightly with salt and pepper. Sauté in batches until nicely browned, but still rare inside. Remove the browned meat and transfer to the dish with the mushrooms and onions.
- **Make the sauce, SIR:** Add the shallots to the pan and sauté for 1 minute. Then add the beef stock, vermouth, cream, nutmeg, and any juice that has collected around the mushrooms, onions, and meat. Boil and reduce the liquid until only ¼ cup remains. Lower heat, stir in the sour cream, and bring to a low simmer. (From this point on, do not allow the sauce to come to a full boil. It will separate.)
- **Construct the stroganoff, SIR:** Fold the beef, mushrooms, and onions into the sauce and simmer for 5 minutes, until heated through.
- **Thank you, SIR, may I have another:** Taste and adjust seasonings as desired. Serve over buttered noodles, rice, or a shingle. Garnish with chopped parsley. Yield: 6 servings.
- **News from the front:** Inform your dining companions that you've suddenly been called off to engage in secret nighttime training maneuvers, and will, most regrettably, be unavailable for KP duty. At ease, soldier.

Food for Thought

Kudos to Bill Murray for finding
a new use for the spatula.
How many can you think of?

Golden Ladyfingers

We think even James Bond would approve of this next recipe. It calls for 3 of his favorite ingredients: liquor, real gold flakes, and ladyfingers.

3 large eggs, separated
½ cup sugar
1 tsp vanilla extract
3 Tbsp Goldschläger liquor (containing real gold flakes), divided
8 oz mascarpone, softened (If this Italian cream cheese is not available, use softened plain cream cheese whipped with 1 Tbsp sour cream)
24 ladyfingers, cut in half crosswise
1 cup cold espresso or strong coffee
1 cup whipping cream
⅛ cup unsweetened cocoa
½ oz white chocolate
1 boxed set of Shirley Bassey's greatest hit . . ."Gold*fingaaaah*"

- Combine the egg yolks, sugar, vanilla, and 2 tablespoons of Goldschläger in a medium mixing bowl. Place the bowl over a saucepan of simmering water and beat until pale yellow, thick, and hot, about 10 minutes. Scrape the mixture into a large bowl, add the mascarpone, and beat until smooth. Beat the egg whites until soft peaks form, and fold gently into the mascarpone mixture.
- Lay out the ladyfingers on a cookie sheet and brush both sides lightly with espresso. Set out 8 martini glasses or wine goblets. Arrange a layer of ladyfingers in each glass; top with a spoonful of the cheese mixture. Repeat with

WARNING: This recipe contains raw egg whites, which usually pose no problem for healthy adults. If serving to anyone very young, very old, or with health problems, please substitute 1 cup of freshly whipped cream for the egg whites.

THINGS YOU NEVER HEAR JAMES BOND SAY:

· No alcohol for me; I'm on antibiotics.

· How much do you think I should tip?

· Excuse me, miss, was it good for you?

another layer of ladyfingers, followed by another spoonful of the cheese mixture. Place the glasses on a tray and freeze 30–45 minutes.

- Whip the cream with 1 tablespoon of Goldschläger and spoon a little over each dessert. Dust with unsweetened cocoa and grate a little white chocolate over each before serving. Yield: 8 servings.
- While you are waiting for the ladyfingers to chill, use the rest of the bottle of Goldschläger and a paintbrush to reenact any favorite scenes from the movie.

INSIDE SCOOP

To create 007's name, Ian Fleming took the first name of one former classmate and the surname of another and merged them to form James Bond.

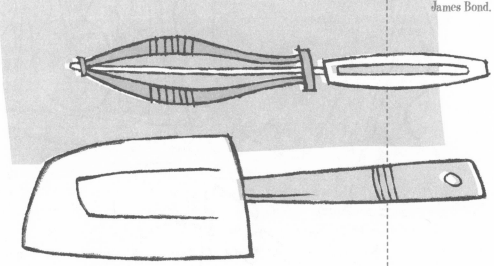

Chew on This The Aston Martin that 007 drove in this movie was sold at Sotheby's in June 1986 for $275,000, the highest price ever paid for a movie prop at auction.

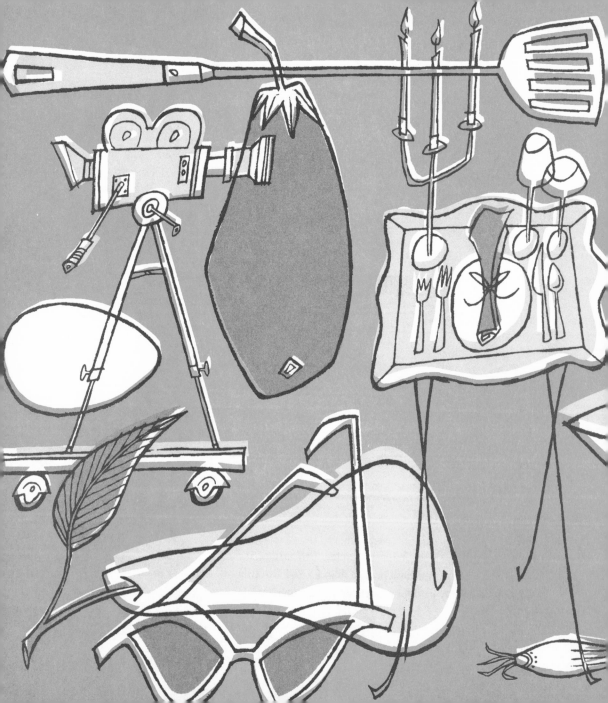

The Loverboy Caesar with Extra Anchovies

Dim the lights, slip into something more comfortable, and oil up your salad tongs. This passionate Caesar really aims to please.

Chew on This

The following is a list of foods that have long been considered aphrodisiacs:

anchovies, pomegranates, watercress, dates, chocolate, pickles, asparagus, and snails (that would explain those yearnings while gardening).

For the Dressing and the Salad

16 anchovy filets
2 egg yolks
2 tsp Dijon mustard
5 cloves garlic, finely chopped
1 tsp freshly ground black pepper
3 Tbsp freshly squeezed lemon juice
1 Tbsp red wine vinegar
2 tsp Worcestershire sauce
1½ cups grated Parmesan cheese
1½ cups pure olive oil
2 Tbsp ice water
4–6 hearts of romaine, rinsed and dried

For the Croutons

2 Tbsp oil from the anchovies
4 Tbsp olive oil
2 cloves garlic
1 tsp fresh thyme, finely chopped
½ tsp salt
½ tsp pepper
2 cups French bread, cut into 1-inch cubes
1 Barry White album

WARNING: This is our version of the classic Caesar salad, which uses raw eggs in the dressing. This generally poses no problem for healthy adults; however, if serving to anyone very old, very young, or with health problems, try substituting 1 tablespoon of mayonnaise for each egg yolk.

- **Make the dressing:** Put on your favorite Barry White album.
- In a medium mixing bowl, mash half of the anchovy filets. Add the egg yolks, mustard, garlic, black pepper, lemon juice, red wine vinegar, Worcestershire, and ½ cup of the grated Parmesan. Slowly and rhythmically whisk all ingredients together. Oh baby.
- Add the olive oil in a slow, steady stream, all the while whisking constantly. If all goes well, the mixture should begin to get thicker and stiffer. Don't stop now; keep it up until all of the oil is consumed in a sexy emulsion. Put a little on your finger and bring it up to your lips. Mmmm.
- If the dressing gets a little too stiff, whisk in a couple of tablespoons of ice water (or think about baseball).
- Cover, refrigerate, and consider having a cigarette. Nah, you quit.
- **Make the croutons:** Combine the anchovy oil, olive oil, garlic, thyme, salt, and pepper in a large skillet and place over medium heat. Add the croutons and stir to coat with the oil. Continue cooking until the croutons begin to turn golden brown, stirring constantly.
- **Watch the Caesar spring to life:** Tear the hearts of romaine into bite-sized pieces or leave whole, depending on your mood.
- Toss the hearts with a ladleful of the dressing, pile onto chilled plates and top with warm croutons, anchovies, and grated Parmesan.
- Take a bite and wait for the flavors to explode in your mouth. Yield: 4 servings.

INSIDE SCOOP
What women really think are aphrodisiacs:
- a clean kitchen
- someone else picking up their dry cleaning
- a shoe organizer
- anyone else cooking dinner
- a great matte lipstick for under 5 bucks

Food for Thought

The moral of this movie is:
1. Love and profit are not mutually exclusive.
2. Free enterprise may land you at the free clinic.

Male Chauvinist Pig

This glass-ceiling favorite is popular with pork lovers everywhere, regardless of gender.

For the Pork Roast
1 3-lb boneless center loin pork roast
¼ tsp ground bay leaf
½ tsp clove
½ tsp ground cinnamon
2 tsp freshly ground black pepper
2 tsp kosher salt
1 Tbsp fresh rosemary, finely chopped
8 cloves garlic, cut into slivers

For the Cabbage
2 Tbsp butter
1 yellow onion, thinly sliced
6 cups red cabbage, shredded
3 Tbsp cider vinegar
3 Tbsp honey (feel free to substitute Skinny & Sweet)
½ cup dark beer
½ cup chicken stock
¼ tsp celery seed
Salt and pepper to taste
4 Tbsp Italian parsley, chopped
1 bottle window cleaner (for glass ceiling)

- Adjust oven rack position to the upper third of the oven and preheat to 475°F.
- **Tie 'em up:** Cut a length of twine about 6 times the length (or height) of the rascal you're about to lasso. Make a slip knot and drop it over the end that's not kicking. Continue by making a series of half hitches until you've used up

Chew on This

Because contemporary pork is no longer bred for lard, it's much more healthful than its plump predecessor. One ounce of lean pork contains about 2 grams of fat–as compared to 16 grams for the same amount of peanut butter. So next time you're hungry for a snack, try a pork-and-jelly sandwich.

your slack. (By this time he may have stopped struggling and will listen to reason. . . . Nah.)

- **Rub it in:** In a small bowl, combine the bay leaf, clove, cinnamon, pepper, salt, and rosemary. Rub spice mixture into meat. If your chauvinist gets suspicious, tell him it's a new blend of Old Spice.
- **Stud the stud with garlic:** Pierce the pork in 15–20 spots with a paring knife or skewer and insert a garlic sliver into each opening.
- **Roast 'em up:** Place the roast on a rack in a roasting pan. Slide the pan into the oven and set the timer for 30 minutes. After 30 minutes, remove the roast from the oven and reduce the oven temperature to 325°F. Allow the oven to cool before returning the meat to the oven (about 20 minutes). Cook for a final 20–30 minutes, to an internal temperature of 150°–155°F. Let rest for 15 minutes before carving.
- **Make the bed:** Melt the butter in a medium saucepan over medium heat. Add the onions and sauté until limp, about 3 minutes. Add the remaining ingredients, cover, and cook for 15–20 minutes. Toss with chopped parsley just before serving. Arrange slices of roast over bed of cabbage. Yield: 6 servings.
- **Savor the moment:** Now you've got your male chauvinist pig just the way you want him: tasteful, submissive, and served on a bed of your own choosing (in this case, cabbage).

Food for Thought

Most popular politically incorrect food names:

honeybun, sugarpie, peaches, peanut, pumpkin, bundt cake, head cheese, pork butt, java drawers.

Pretty Woman
Angel Hair Puttanesca

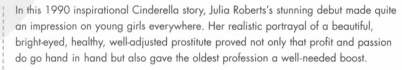

In this 1990 inspirational Cinderella story, Julia Roberts's stunning debut made quite an impression on young girls everywhere. Her realistic portrayal of a beautiful, bright-eyed, healthy, well-adjusted prostitute proved not only that profit and passion do go hand in hand but also gave the oldest profession a well-needed boost.

⅓ cup extra virgin olive oil
1 onion, chopped
1 carrot, cut in a small dice
4 garlic cloves, minced
6 anchovy filets, rinsed and mashed
¼ tsp crushed red pepper
½ cup dry red wine
3 lbs ripe tomatoes or 1 28-oz can peeled plum tomatoes, drained and chopped
1½ cups flavorful black olives, pitted and halved
3 Tbsp large capers, drained
Salt and pepper
1 lb angel hair pasta
Hugh Grant's phone number

- Heat the olive oil in a medium saucepan over medium-low heat. Add the onion and carrot and cook very slowly until the onion becomes soft and translucent, about 10 minutes. Add the garlic, anchovies, and crushed red pepper; continue cooking until the garlic just begins to turn golden. (Don't let it brown.)
- Add the red wine and raise the heat to medium-high. Simmer until the wine has almost reduced completely. Stir in the tomatoes, olives, and capers. Reduce heat to medium and cook, uncovered, for 20 minutes, stirring often. (While the sauce simmers, bring 5–6 quarts of water to a boil in a large pot or Dutch oven.)
- When the sauce has thickened, stir in the chopped parsley and season to taste

Chew on This

TOMATO TIPS
#87 & 88

• Never store tomatoes in the refrigerator for any length of time. Cold temperatures hurt both the texture and the flavor.

• If ripe tomatoes aren't available, never hesitate to use good-quality canned Italian plum tomatoes.

with salt and pepper. Add more red pepper flakes if desired.

- When the water boils, add 2 tablespoons of salt and return to a boil. Add the pasta all at once and stir immediately to prevent sticking. Cover the pot just until the water returns to a boil again; then uncover and cook until pasta is *al dente*, stirring often.
- Drain pasta into a colander over a large pasta bowl. Dump out the water and wipe the bowl with a towel before transferring the pasta to the warmed bowl. Immediately ladle the sauce over the pasta. Toss and serve in shallow bowls. Yield: 4–6 servings.

Historical Tidbit: **Ever hear of "the oldest profession"? According to many historians, it's cooking. (The second oldest is dishwashing.)**

INSIDE SCOOP

A rumored early version of the script had the Richard Gere character end the relationship with the Julia Roberts character by throwing her out of his car, driving off, and leaving her with only one option: She and her prostitute friend end up on a bus to Disneyland. Fade to black.

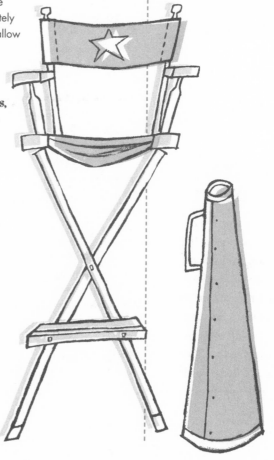

INSIDE SCOOP

Rumor has it the working title was originally *$3,000.*

Wildcatfish with
Homemade BBQ Sauce & Slaw

Okay, team. If Goldie Hawn can get the job done, so can you. As a high school football coach, she led her rag-tag team to victory against insurmountable odds. All you have to do is huddle up with your ingredients and follow the recipe. So get out there and cook! Go! Go! Go! (At this point feel free to pat each ingredient on the butt as you place it on the counter.)

For the Barbeque Sauce
4 Tbsp butter
4 cloves garlic, finely chopped
1 medium onion, diced
1 tsp paprika
6 Tbsp brown sugar
½ tsp instant coffee
1 tsp dry mustard
¼ tsp cayenne pepper
1 tsp freshly ground black pepper
1 tsp salt
2 Tbsp lemon juice
1 Tbsp soy sauce
½ cup catsup
1 tsp sesame oil
½ tsp hot pepper sauce
½ cup orange juice
1 cup tomato sauce
¼ cup cider vinegar
½ cup beer

For the Slaw
½ cup slivered almonds
½ tsp celery seed
1 tsp mustard seed
3 Tbsp rice vinegar
½ cup pure olive oil
¼ head red cabbage, thinly sliced
3 ears corn, kernels cut from the cob
2 ripe beefsteak tomatoes, diced
¼ cup cilantro, roughly chopped
Salt and freshly ground pepper

For the Wildcatfish
3 Tbsp peanut oil
4 6–8-oz catfish filets
2 Tbsp all-purpose flour
3 cups athletic cups

Food for Thought

Cat lovers, relax. The phrase "more than one way to skin a cat" refers to catfish, not kitty cats, and is probably a reference to the difficulty in skinning the little suckers. Some people even use pliers.

- **Prepare the BBQ sauce:** In a medium saucepan, melt the butter and sauté the onions and garlic until soft and golden. While the onions and garlic cook, combine, in two separate bowls, the dry ingredients and the wet ingredients.
- Add the mixture of dry ingredients to the saucepan and cook for one minute, stirring constantly. Add the combined wet ingredients and mix well. Let the sauce come to a boil; reduce the heat and simmer for 30–45 minutes.
- **Make the slaw:** Preheat the oven to 350°F. Spread the almond slivers on a cookie sheet and bake 10–15 minutes, or until light brown. (Leave oven on to bake fish.)
- In a small mixing bowl, combine the toasted almonds, celery seed, mustard seed, rice vinegar, and olive oil.
- In a large salad bowl, toss together the red cabbage, corn, tomatoes, and cilantro; add the dressing and toss again. Season with salt and pepper to taste.
- **Cook the Wildcatfish:** Heat the peanut oil in a large, heavy skillet on medium-high heat until a light haze appears above the oil. Dust the catfish with the flour, shake off any excess, and lay smooth-side up in the hot skillet. Cook for 2 minutes; flip the catfish over and brush a little barbecue sauce over each filet. Transfer skillet to the preheated oven and bake 5 minutes.
- Serve the catfish over a mound of slaw, smother with sauce, and eat rapidly. Yield: **4 servings.**
- When you've made it all the way through the recipe and emerged victorious, throw down your oven mitt and perform a spirited touchdown victory dance! (Headbutting of dinner guests is optional.)

Chew on This

Goldie Hawn won an Academy Award for Best Supporting Actress for her role in *Cactus Flower* (1969), her first film.

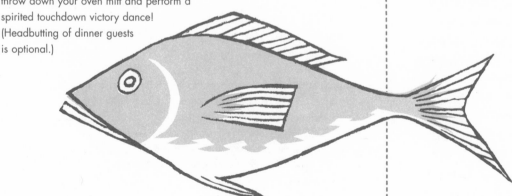

Pigs-in-a-Blanket

The mission is to protect and serve dinner. You have the right to remain in the kitchen; you have the right to an apron. If you don't have an apron, we can provide you with one. Anything you burn can and will be used against you.

For the Pigs

2 pork tenderloins, trimmed
2 tsp freshly ground black pepper
2 tsp fresh thyme, chopped
8 cloves garlic, chopped
1½ Tbsp whole mustard seed, crushed
¼ tsp ground allspice
¼ tsp ground cinnamon
1 tsp salt
1 Tbsp Dijon mustard
4 Tbsp pure olive oil

For the Bed

2 Tbsp butter
2 medium yellow onions, thinly sliced
2 Rome Beauty apples, thinly sliced
2 Granny Smith apples, thinly sliced

1 cup white wine (dry Gewürztraminer
    or Riesling is nice)
¼ cup cider vinegar
2 Tbsp sugar
1 tsp kosher salt
½ tsp caraway seed
3 sprigs of fresh thyme

For the Blankets

1 16-oz box frozen puff pastry or
    croissant dough, defrosted
1 egg yolk mixed with 1 Tbsp water
Lots of glazed doughnuts and coffee
    (a guy's gotta keep his strength up)

- **Prepare the pigs:** Preheat oven to 425°F. Round up and apprehend the ingredients. In a small bowl, combine and make a paste of the pepper, thyme, garlic, mustard seed, allspice, cinnamon, salt, mustard, and 2 tablespoons of the olive oil. Rub the paste well into the pork tenderloins.
- Heat a large skillet or sauté pan on medium-high heat until quite hot. Add the remaining olive oil. When the oil just begins to smoke, add the meat and brown well on all sides. Remove the tenderloins from the pan and set aside to cool before wrapping.

Food for Thought

Many cookbooks recommend cooking pork to an internal temperature of 180°F for safety. Because the trichinae parasites cannot survive temperatures above 140°F, we feel that cooking to a temperature of 165°F will produce pork that is safe, yet still tender and moist.

- **Make the bed:** Add 2 tablespoons of butter to the hot pan along with the onions and apples and sauté until softened. Add the wine to the apples and onions and scrape pan with a wooden spoon to loosen any browned bits. Allow the wine to cook down by half, then add the vinegar, sugar, salt, caraway seed, and thyme sprigs. Simmer until most of the liquid is gone and the onions and apples are tender and moist. Remove from heat, cover, and keep warm.
- **Tuck in the blanket:** Open puff pastry and lay out one piece flat on a clean, dry cutting board. If necessary, dust with a little flour, then roll out to create a rectangle large enough to wrap one tenderloin. Brush inside edges of the puff pastry with the egg mixture. Lay one tenderloin in the center of the pastry, bring ends of the pastry dough to meet at the top and crimp well to seal. Fold and crimp both ends and place seam-side down on a foil-lined cookie sheet. Brush all over with the egg mixture. Repeat process with the second tenderloin.
- Make three diagonal cuts on top of each cozy pig and decorate with little dough cutouts of bullets, billy clubs, and doughnuts. Bake in the top half of the oven for 15–20 minutes or until lightly browned.
- Let the pigs rest for 5 minutes while you finish your doughnut and coffee.
- Slice diagonally and serve lying on the bed of braised apples and onions. Yield: 4 servings.

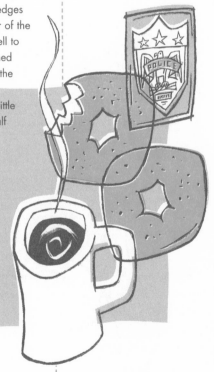

Chew on This

This send-up spawned 6 sequels and a television series.

Food for Thought

Was Steve Guttenburg solely responsible for the popularity of crop-top T-shirts, shorty shorts, and tube socks?

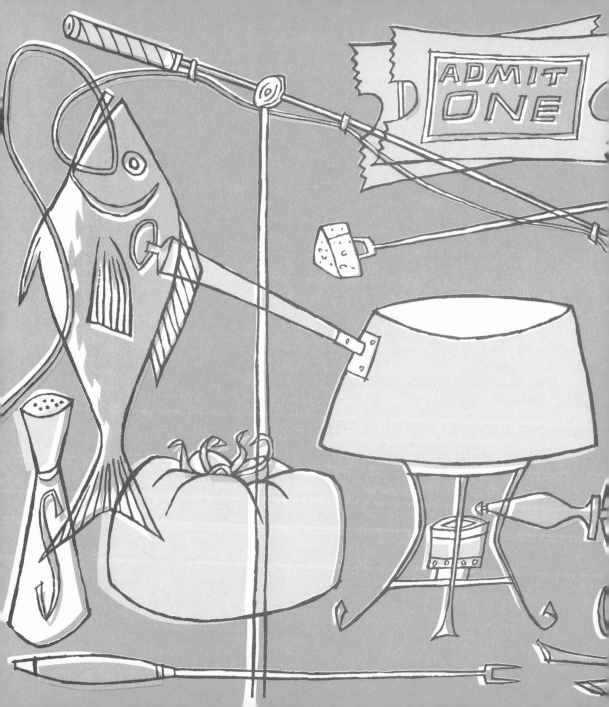

Home On the Range

Classic Cul de Sac Mac 'n' Cheese

... or as we like to call it, Dr. Klopeck's What's-That-Smell-In-the-Basement Hackaroni Casserole.

For the Cheese Sauce

3 cups whole milk
½ onion
1 bay leaf
2 whole cloves
½ cup butter
¼ cup shallots, minced
⅓ cup flour
1 tsp dry mustard
⅛ tsp white pepper
1 Tbsp Worcestershire sauce
⅛ tsp nutmeg
⅛ tsp cayenne
1 tsp chopped fresh thyme
½ tsp salt

For the Filling

16 oz dry macaroni
1½ cups grated Gruyère or Swiss cheese
2 cups grated cheddar cheese
1½ cups grated Parmesan cheese
½ cup bread crumbs
1 "Kiss the Cook" apron
1 set lawn darts
1 box of grass seed
1 dirty little secret

Chew on This

Tom Hanks was the first actor to win back-to-back Academy Awards for Best Actor since Spencer Tracy did it in 1937 and 1938. Hanks won his for *Philadelphia* and *Forrest Gump*.

- Preheat oven to 375°F. Butter a 3-quart casserole.
- Cook the macaroni *al dente* (a minute or two less than the package instructions may call for). Rinse in cold water, drain, and set aside.
- **Make the cheese sauce:** Pour the milk into a small saucepan. Tack the bay leaf to the onion with the cloves and place in the milk. Slowly bring the milk to a simmer on medium heat.
- Melt ¼ cup of butter in a medium saucepan over medium heat. Add the chopped shallots and cook until soft. Add the flour, dry mustard, and white pepper and cook another 3 minutes, stirring often.
- Slowly add the hot milk to the butter and flour mixture, whisking constantly. Stir in the Worcestershire; transfer the clove-studded onion and simmer at least 20 minutes (stirring occasionally), until sauce is thick and creamy.
- Remove from heat, discard the onion, and stir in ½ cup each of the grated cheddar and Gruyère. Whisk in the fresh thyme, nutmeg, cayenne, and salt.
- **Mix and bake:** Turn the cooked, drained macaroni into the buttered casserole, add the hot cheese sauce, and stir together. Stir in ½ cup of the Parmesan and the remaining cheddar and Gruyère.
- Sprinkle with the rest of the Parmesan cheese and the bread crumbs; dot with the remaining butter and bake uncovered in the upper third of the preheated oven for 30 minutes, or until brown and bubbly. Yield: 8 servings.

Suburban Psycho Safety Tip:

Remember, if you run out of something and decide to pop over and borrow stuff from your neighbors instead of making a trip to the market, you may end up with much more than just a cup of milk. Howdy neighbor, we've been expecting you!

"Fall Apart" Pot Roast

Unlike the dream house turned nightmare in this 1986 Steven Spielberg production, our pot roast is designed and constructed to fall apart.

5 lbs boneless chuck roast
¼ cup brandy
2–3 tsp kosher salt
2 tsp freshly ground black pepper
1 tsp paprika
2 tsp garlic powder
½ tsp crushed thyme
2½ Tbsp all-purpose flour
3 Tbsp olive oil
1 cup roughly chopped onions
1 cup roughly chopped carrots
1 cup roughly chopped celery
2 cups roughly chopped leeks
6 cloves garlic, sliced thinly
2 cups tomatoes, roughly chopped
2 cups dry red wine
2 cups beef stock
6 parsley sprigs
1 bay leaf
3 whole cloves
4 sprigs fresh thyme
8 whole black peppercorns
10–12 small new potatoes, cut in half
1 hardhat
1 large second mortage

Chew on This

Typically, cuts of meat used in pot roasting are high in collagen, a tough connective protein that dissolves and turns to gelatin only when subjected to long periods of moist heat.

- Rinse roast with cold water and pat dry with paper towels. Place in a large bowl and rub well with the brandy.
- Using a series of half-hitches, tie the roast firmly with butcher's twine. If knots make you nuts, ask the butcher for a meat wrap. They're usually free.
- Mix together the salt, pepper, paprika, garlic powder, thyme, and flour. Rub the mixture into roast.
- Heat the olive oil in a large Dutch oven or heavy pot over medium-high heat until almost smoking. Place roast in the hot oil and brown well on each side, about 12–15 minutes total. Transfer the roast to a plate.
- Add the chopped vegetables, garlic, and tomatoes and sauté 5–10 minutes. Add the red wine and use a wooden spoon to scrape loose any tasty browned bits stuck to the pan.
- Cook the red wine down by half; add the parsley, bay leaf, fresh thyme, and peppercorns. Return the meat to the pot.
- Bring to a very low simmer. Cover tightly and cook either over a low heat or in an oven preheated to 200°F for 4–5 hours, turning the meat every half hour. Add the potatoes 1 hour before serving.
  Important: Never allow the roast to come to a full boil. Boiling will dry out the meat.
- Remove the meat and potatoes to a warm platter and cover. Spoon off any grease floating on the surface of the pot juices. Transfer half of the remaining vegetables to a blender and blend well; return the blended vegetables to the pot and cook down a few minutes over high heat until thickened. Ladle gravy over meat and serve at once. Yield: 6 servings.
- Pretend you're a general contractor! Tell your guests dinner will be served at 6 P.M. sharp and that you would like a five-dollar donation toward the groceries. Then don't serve dinner until midnight and charge them each forty dollars plus labor!

Shrunken Shanks with Pygmy Veggies in Red Wine Reduction Sauce

This is proof positive that shrinking is not always a bad thing. It inspired this recipe, which is big on taste and made Rick Moranis realize that happiness was right there at home in his bowl of cereal.

4 lamb shanks
4 cloves garlic, each cut in 6 slivers
2 tsp grated lemon zest
2 tsp kosher salt
2 tsp freshly ground black pepper
½ tsp sugar
½ cup lemon juice
4 Tbsp pure olive oil
3 Tbsp flour
½ cup roughly chopped yellow onion
½ cup roughly chopped celery
½ cup roughly chopped carrot
1 Tbsp tomato paste
1 cup pinot noir (or other tasty medium-bodied red wine)
½ cup peeled, seeded, and chopped tomato
1 bay leaf
¼ bunch parsley sprigs, tied together with string
1 lb assorted baby vegetables (red potatoes, carrots, zucchini, yellow squash, etc.)
1 magnifying glass

- Rinse shanks in cold water, dry, and trim off excess fat. Using a sharp paring knife, cut six slits in the meatiest parts of each shank, inserting a garlic sliver in each slit as you go.
- Mix together lemon zest, salt, pepper, sugar, 1 tablespoon of the olive oil, and ¼

INSIDE SCOOP

A large proportion of the lamb imported to the U.S. is from New Zealand, where sheep outnumber people 20 to 1.

Food for Thought

Many of the "baby" vegetables available today are actually full-grown, miniature, hybrid vegetables.

cup of the lemon juice. Rub this mixture well into meat. Cover and refrigerate for 20 minutes, while preparing and assembling the remaining ingredients.

- Heat the remaining olive oil in a large, thick-bottomed pot on medium-high heat. Remove the lamb shanks from the marinade and blot dry with a paper towel; dust with flour and sear on all sides for about 5 minutes, until nicely browned. Transfer the browned shanks to a plate and set aside. Pour off all but 2 table-spoons of the fat and add the onion, celery, carrot, and tomato paste. Sauté this mixture for 2–3 minutes and then add the remaining lemon juice, wine, tomato, bay leaf, and parsley.

- Return the meat to the pot, along with any juices on the plate. Bring to a simmer; reduce heat to low and cook covered for at least 2 hours, until meat is very tender and succulent.

- Add the baby vegetables during the last 30 minutes of cooking. Remove the meat and vegetables to a warm platter, cover, and keep warm.

- Spoon off and discard any fat floating on the top of the pot juices, bring to a boil and reduce to a gravy-like consistency. Season to taste with salt and pepper.

- Ladle the red wine reduction over the pygmy veggies and shrunken shanks; eat rapidly. Yield: 4 servings.

- Remember, there are no small meals, only small cooks.

Chew on This

"Ze parent-child relationship is directly linked to ze size of ze vegetables you feed zem."

—Dr. Sigmund Child,
The Galloping Shrink

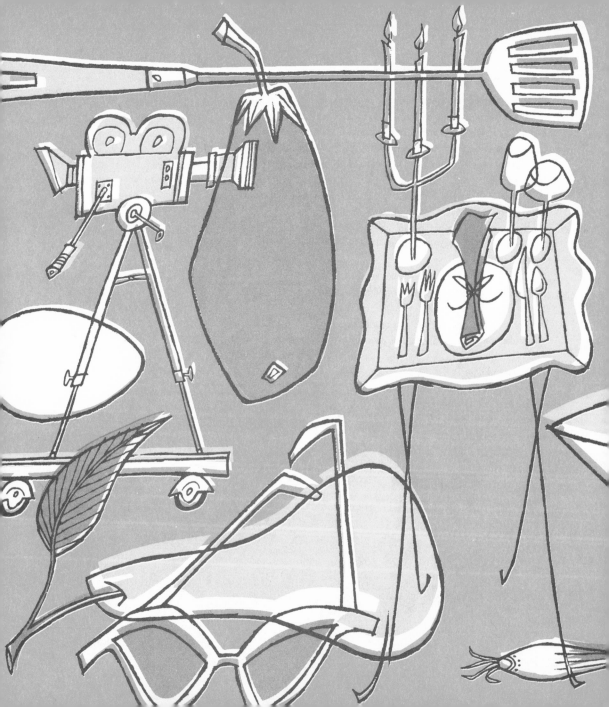

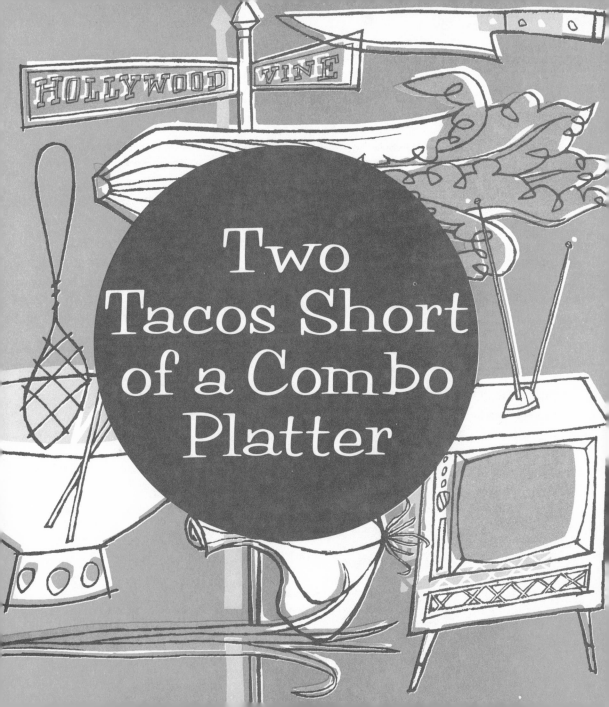

Two
Tacos Short
of a Combo
Platter

Soup-on-a-Stick

You don't have to be the sharpest tool in the shed to make a darn good soup on a stick. Just try to follow this simple recipe and look up any big words.

For the Soup:

1 lb large shrimp
4 lbs chicken backs and necks
2 thin slices fresh ginger
½ tsp black peppercorns
2 scallions, cut into 2-inch pieces
3 cloves garlic, peeled and crushed
¼ cup dried mushrooms (optional)
4 qts cold water
1 tsp salt

For the Stick:

1 lb beef tenderloin, well trimmed
1 lb pork tenderloin, well trimmed
1 lb skinless, boneless chicken breasts
8 oz firm tofu
1 English cucumber, cut in ¾-inch cubes
6 scallions, cut in 2-inch pieces

For Service:

3 Tbsp soy sauce
2 Tbsp sesame oil
1 tsp chili paste
2 tsp white vinegar
½ napa cabbage, sliced thinly
½ lb baby spinach, stems removed
In case of dumb kitchen accidents: 1 phone book to look up the number for 911

> "I love California.
> I practically grew up
> in Phoenix."
>
> —Vice President Dan Quayle

INSIDE SCOOP

When a recipe calls for very thin slices of meat or chicken, try freezing it partially for an hour of so. Slicing will be much easier.

- **Try to make the soup:** Peel and devein the shrimp. Arrange on a platter, cover, and refrigerate. Combine shrimp shells with the chicken backs, ginger, peppercorns, scallions, garlic, and mushrooms in a large, heavy pot. Cover with cold water and bring to a rapid boil over high heat. Skim the surface to remove any scum that floats to the top. Partially cover the pot, reduce heat, and cook at a low simmer for at least 1 hour, preferably 2. Strain liquid through a fine strainer into a large bowl; skim off any fat that rises to the top; salt to taste and set aside. **Important:** avoid submerging head or extremities in the broth until it has cooled.

- **Try not to hurt yourself:** Slice the beef, pork, and chicken breasts across the grain as thinly as possible and arrange on a platter. (When slicing the meats, may we suggest a knife?)

- In a small bowl, make a sauce by mixing together the soy sauce, sesame oil, chili paste, and vinegar. In a medium serving bowl, toss together the napa cabbage and spinach.

- **Try to serve dinner:** Place an electric skillet or wok in the center of the table and bring the broth to a simmer. Arrange the uncooked foods around the simmering broth and ask the dumbest person present to please come forward. (If everyone steps forward, pick the person with the cleanest hands.) Explain slowly and clearly that he or she has the great honor of preparing the soup for everyone and that you're genuinely sorry they won't have the time to eat.

- Have Mr. Lucky begin preparing the skewers by alternating the tofu, cucumber, and scallions with little rolled-up slices of each meat on each skewer (draw a simple diagram if necessary). Submerge the skewers in the simmering broth just long enough to cook the meat, about 2 minutes.

- Using a fork, push the cooked meat and vegetables off the skewers and into soup bowls. Put a handful of the cabbage and spinach mixture in each bowl. Top with a ladleful of hot broth and a dollop of the chili-soy sauce.

Yield: 6–8 servings.

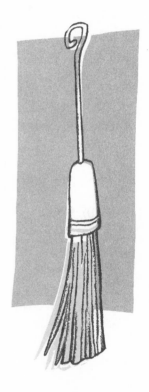

Food for Thought Did you know this movie made $206,170 in the Czech Republic and $127,000,000 in the United States?

Big Jerked Chicken

Although this chicken was raised by a family of poor blackbirds, it managed to pull itself out of poverty and right into your oven.

For the Jerk Seasoning

⅓ cup cider vinegar

1 Tbsp molasses

1 Tbsp soy sauce

1 Tbsp Worcestershire sauce

Juice and zest of 1 lime

1 tsp light brown sugar

4 Tbsp softened butter

4 scallions, chopped

3 cloves garlic, peeled

¼ tsp black pepper

1 tsp salt

2 tsp ground cinnamon

2 tsp ground allspice

1 Tbsp peeled and thinly sliced fresh ginger

1 habanero pepper (aka Scotch bonnet), or 2–3 jalapeños, seeded

For the Chicken

1 4–5 lb chicken

1 thumb-sized piece of ginger, sliced thinly

1 whole head garlic, cut in half

1 lime, cut in quarters

1 habanero or jalapeño, halved lengthwise

1 pair opti-grabs

- **Prepare the jerk:** Measure out and combine all jerk seasoning ingredients in the work bowl of a food processor or blender. Blend until smooth.

INSIDE SCOOP

The practice of breaking the wishbone to see who gets the larger half dates back more than 2,000 years. It is most likely the origin of "a lucky break."

- **Prepare the chicken:** Adjust oven rack to the center of the oven and preheat to 450°F. Rinse and dry the chicken; massage ½ of the the jerk seasoning all over the chicken, under the breast skin, and inside the cavity. Place the ginger, garlic, lime, and habanero inside the cavity and close by tying the ends of the drumsticks together loosely.
- Set the chicken with the breast-side down on an oiled rack in a roasting pan. Roast uncovered for 30 minutes, brushing with pan juices and jerk seasoning every 10 minutes or so. If the pan juices sizzle too loudly or begin to smoke, add ½ cup of water to the pan.
- Flip the chicken breast-side up and reduce the oven temperature to 350°F. Continue roasting an additional hour, basting frequently. The chicken is done when the skin is crisp and brown and the drumsticks feel loose in their sockets. A meat thermometer inserted into the thick part of the thigh nearest the body should register 165°–175°F. Transfer chicken to a platter or carving board and let rest for 15–20 minutes before serving.
- While the chicken rests, transfer the pan juices to a small saucepan and skim off the fat. Remove the garlic and habanero from the cavity, chop finely, and combine with the pan juices. Heat to a simmer and serve alongside the chicken. Yield: 4 servings.

Chew on This

Steve Martin got his start by selling 25-cent guidebooks and entertaining at Disneyland.

Know Your Terms!

Beat 1) to vigorously stir to blend ingredients 2) the pregnant pauses between the very important lines an actor has and the stuff the other actors say.

Beefcake 1) pastry-encased meat of a bovine animal 2) well-muscled actor who finds himself shirtless more often than not.

Blanch 1) to cook briefly in a liquid medium 2) best-known Tennessee Williams character, who claimed to depend on the kindness of strangers.

Blend in 1) to combine and mix ingredients well 2) what an extra does if he wants to keep working.

Butterfly 1) to split open and spread apart 2a) particularly embarrassing Pia Zadora vehicle 2b) something that forms in actors' stomachs prior to their walking on stage and forgetting their lines.

Caper 1) the pickled bud of the caper bush 2) popular genre of action-adventure movie.

Chafing 1) type of dish used to keep food hot at the table 2) painful condition suffered by actors working in adult films and westerns.

Cheesy 1) dish using cheese as a key ingredient 2) movie containing an overabundance of unnaturally belabored saccharine moments.

Coddle 1) to gently cook in very hot, but not boiling, water 2) how a star actor is treated regardless of their behavior.

Corny 1) dish employing large amounts of corn 2) much like Cheesy, but less believable.

Cottage Cheese 1) a fresh, unripened cheese 2) good reason for use of a body double.

Curdling 1) denaturing process caused by enzymes, acidity, or heat whereby milk separates and turns to curd 2) type of spine-tingling, high-pitched scream employed by actresses in horror movies.

Cut 1) to divide into pieces with the use of a sharp tool 2) what the director shouts to stop the cameras from rolling.

Demi-Glace 1) a very highly reduced meat stock 2a) lipstick specifically formulated to be used under bright lights 2b) former name of mysteriously successful actress before having changed her last name to Moore.

Dice 1) to cut food into small uniform cubes 2) clever middle name of former stand-up comedian turned actor (see also Hack).

Emulsion 1) a mixture composed of a suspension of fat globules 2) light-sensitive coating on movie film that causes it to capture and retain an image.

Flake 1) to break apart into small pieces 2) to forget to show up for rehearsal.

Fold 1) to combine ingredients with a gentle, circular motion 2) what generally happens to a show after unanimously scathing reviews.

Fool 1) English dessert consisting of fruit folded into whipping cream or custard 2) word most used by stockholders when describing the studio executive who passed on *E.T.*

Gel 1) to congeal with the use of gelatin or pectin 2) color filter used over stage lighting.

Ginger 1) aromatic rhizome commonly used in Asian cooking 2a) the one you chose over Mary Ann 2b) the one you chose over Cyd Charisse.

Glaze 1) to brush with a light coating of sauce 2a) look commonly seen in the eyes of Hollywood agents when discussing large amounts of money 2b) official doughnut of the teamster's union, Hollywood local.

Grate 1) to cut food into small bits with the use of a grater 2) the effect that actors crossing over into singing careers have on the ears of the hearing.

Grease 1) to wipe fat onto a pan to keep food from sticking to it 2) incredibly popular musical starring middle-aged teenage actors.

Grind 1) to reduce into powder by crushing between hard surfaces 2a) highly specialized acting technique used by actresses appearing in any film by Joe Eszterhaus 2b) how a $300,000-a-week television actor describes his job after a grueling two seasons.

Hack 1) to forcefully cut with uneven or irregular blows 2) an actor who's either been seen in more than one infomercial, or should be.

Ham 1) the cured thigh or hind leg of a hog or pig 2) actor who can't differentiate on-stage from off-.

Junket 1) a rennet-thickened, milk-based dessert 2) an all-expenses-paid vacation for the Hollywood press corps in which they're allowed to follow a star around and ask probing and insightful questions.

Loins 1) the tender cuts of meat taken from the front quarter of an animal on either side of the backbone 2) common spot for aching to be felt by characters in the "coming of age" film genre.

Mace 1) popular baking spice found in the outer layer of the fruit of the nutmeg tree 2) popular defensive aerosol used by actresses to keep frisky paparazzi at bay.

Mint 1) any of several aromatic herbs belonging to the mint family 2) cost of an average Kevin Costner spectacle.

Mole 1) famous Mexican sauce containing, among other things, chiles, chocolate, garlic, and sesame seeds 2) trademark facial imperfection.

Mousse 1) dish consisting of a flavoring base folded into whipped cream or egg whites 2) gooey hair product very popular with moody young actors appearing in John Hughes movies.

Pasties 1) little meat-and-vegetable turnovers 2) the difference between an "R" or an "NC17" rating.

Pearl Barley 1) a highly polished form of barley commonly used in soup 2) highly polished singer commonly seen in old movies.

Roll 1) a small, rounded individual portion of bread 2) what the director shouts to begin filming.

Saccharin 1) non-caloric sugar substitute approximately 500 times sweeter than sugar 2) a shameless display of insincere emotion.

Score 1) to partially cut through the outer surface of a food 2) written musical composition that, when recorded, becomes part of the soundtrack of a film.

Season 1) to enhance the taste of food through the use of spices, herbs, etc. 2) a recurrent or specific division of time marked by new film and television releases.

Shark 1) family of edible predatory fish growing up to forty feet in length 2) See Agent below.

Shot 1) one jigger full of alcoholic spirits 2) one in a series of camera angles.

Spit 1) metal rod used to skewer and cook food over an open flame 2) foamy liquid often found issuing forth from the mouths of emotionally charged actors.

Skin 1) to remove the external membranous tissue from a piece of fish or poultry 2) the weaker the script, the more of this you're likely to see.

Thickening Agent 1) any of various ingredients used to thicken sauces, soups, etc. 2) an actor's representative after too many power lunches.

Index

Index

Index

Index

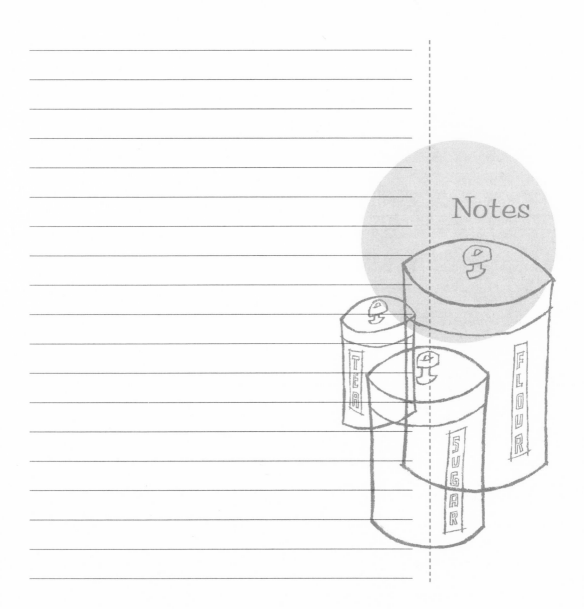

Notes

Notes

Notes

Credits and Acknowledgments

Illustrations by Robert Clyde Anderson
Recipes by Claud Mann
Written by Kimberlee Carlson, Claud Mann, and Robert Taylor

Additional text—Paul Gilmartin, Annabelle Gurwitch, Tom Dorfmeister, Ashley Evans,
Gianna Messina, Lennye Starr, Tim D. Brown, and Kelly Cole.

Special thanks to Bill Burke, Jeff Carr, Bill Cox, Judy Hackett, Alex Kaminsky,
Trish Strong-Harris, Angela Wells, Richard Turner, Will Blair, Ted Cotsen,
Kim Hyatt, Brad Schultz, Matt Walker, I Li Chen, BPS, Allison Strine, Chris Barber,
Kara Jones, Brian Morrow, Editworks, Seth Cohen, Terry Simpson, Perla & Eva Batalla-Mann,
Rick & Lynn Batalla, Hillary & Bobbie Carlson, Bob Hawley, Kevin Bembry,
Ed & Julie Valfre, Heather Johnson, Heidi Taylor.

Designer—Carol Farrar Norton   Editor—Katherine Buttler

Dinner & a Movie
P.O. Box 512
Atlanta, Ga. 30301
http://www.turner.com/dinnermovie

Dinner & a Movie On-Air Production:
Executive Producer—Kimberlee Carlson, Producer—Ashley Evans

Dinner & a Movie on The Superstation TBS
Every Friday night 8:05 P.M. Eastern/5:05 P.M. Pacific
A Second Helping of Dinner & a Movie directly follows
around 10-ish on the East Coast, 7-ish on the West.

Quotes on pp. 30 and 76 from:
Roth, K. Madsen, ed. *Hollywood Wits.* New York: Avon Books, 1995.